The Pearl

Crofts Classics

GENERAL EDITORS

Samuel H. Beer, *Harvard University*
O. B. Hardison, Jr., *Georgetown University*

ANONYMOUS

The Pearl

MEDIAEVAL TEXT AND NOTES BY

Sara deFord
GOUCHER COLLEGE

WITH VERSE TRANSLATION BY

Sara deFord
Dale Elliman Balfour
Donna Rosenbaum Blaustein
Myrna Davidov
Clarinda Harriss Lott
Evelyn Dyke Schroedl

Harlan Davidson, Inc.
Arlington Heights, Illinois 60004

MANUFACTURED IN THE UNITED STATES OF AMERICA

91 90 89 88 87 7 8 9 10 11 TS

PREFACE

✻

The present translation of *The Pearl* was prepared by
an English teacher of Goucher College and a group of
alumnae, her former students. We worked on the transla-
tion in our leisure time for a period of over two years and
hoped to provide a new poetic version for the use of
future English students and for the pleasure of the gen-
eral reader.

As translators, we believed that this mediaeval poem
should be presented to the modern reader in as nearly as
possible its original form. We have tried to keep the trans-
lation close to the sense and the ambiguity of the original.
In style, the poem was, even in its own century, old-
fashioned in its use of the alliterative line, and the dialect
used was remote from that of London. Without deliber-
ately archaizing, we have allowed some archaism to re-
main, in vocabulary and in syntax. With few transpositions,
the translation is line by line. When we have omitted
alliteration, varied the rhyme for sense (or vice versa),
or transposed lines, we have pointed out these changes in
the notes. In various disputes about text and interpreta-
tion, we have presented the major proposals briefly in the
notes and made our choice when choice was essential.
Since scholars differ about the text and the interpretation,
and earlier translators differ in their theories of translation,
we cannot hope to please all readers. In fidelity to the
beauty of the Middle English *Pearl*, we have tried, also,
to write an effective and beautiful poem in modern Eng-
lish. Knowing that we cannot have completely succeeded,
one of the translators remarked at our last session that

"the readers must go back to the original." We hope that they will do so, especially since in this volume it has been facilitated by the presentation of the mediaeval text on the page facing the translation.

Our thanks are due to the Library of Goucher College for lending us indefinitely its collection of texts and translations for *The Pearl* and to the Library of the College of St. Elizabeth for lending us the photostat of the manuscript used by Sister Mary Vincent Hillman. We are grateful for the conscientious and useful line-by-line suggestions of Professor Marie P. Hamilton in the first sixty stanzas, although we were unable to accept without qualification her interpretation of the poem, or her view of the task of translators as interpreters of controversial work. For these faults, if faults they be, and for others (we are painfully aware of many), we fully accept our responsibility. We are appreciative of the constant interest and encouragement offered by the members of the Goucher College community—students, staff, and faculty, and especially of the comments and suggestions of Dean Elizabeth Geen, which have contributed greatly to the initiation of the project in the form in which it now appears.

MIDDLE ENGLISH TEXT

In the manuscript the poem is written without punctuation; capitalization is restricted to the first letter of each five-stanza group (not including group XV, which, comprised of six stanzas, has an initial letter for stanza 81 and another for stanza 82); and stanzas and stanza groups are not separated, spaced, or numbered.

For the convenience of the modern reader, we have spaced the stanzas, numbered them in Arabic, indicated the five-stanza groups with Roman numerals, and numbered the lines of the poem. We have capitalized the first letter of each line, the proper names, and the pronoun "I." Although we have supplied punctuation in the translation, we have left the Middle English text as it is in the

manuscript; we discovered that other editors have sup-
plied varied marks of punctuation which indicate a pre-
ferred meaning, but we wished to allow the reader to see
that our punctuation is not necessarily correct. The au-
thor's spelling was inconsistent. He used both þ and *th;* he
used ʒ for several sounds, as well as *s, z, gh,* etc. He in-
terchanged *i/y* and *u/v.* In our transcription, we have fol-
lowed his usage as carefully as possible. For part of the
work, Mrs. Balfour examined the manuscript in London;
for the work as a whole, we used the photostat, which is
rather difficult to decipher in places.

NOTES

We have found the glossaries and notes in the Os-
good, Gordon, and Hillman editions invaluable and we
have made frequent use of the literal prose translation by
Sister Mary Vincent Hillman. We referred also to the
"Review of Edition by Sister Mary Vincent Hillman" by
Henry L. Savage; to articles by O. F. Emerson, E. M.
Wright, A. C. Cawley, and Sir Israel Gollancz (see Se-
lected Bibliography); and to Professor Hamilton's com-
ments on the translation.

The numbers preceding the notes indicate the line
numbers. Where the manuscript reading is difficult or
disputed, or where differing definitions of a word are
given in the glossaries we have consulted, we have pre-
sented the variations. We have also supplied some notes
to indicate our problems in the translation regarding
rhymes, alliteration, and meter, as well as interpretation.

The abbreviations used in the Notes are the follow-
ing:

> O —Osgood, his edition
> G —Gordon, his edition
> H —Hillman, her edition
> L —Latin
> OE —Old English

ON —Old Norse
ME —Middle English
NE —New English
OED—Oxford English Dictionary
NED—New English Dictionary
MS —manuscript
lit. —literally
l.   —line, ll.—lines

Sara deFord
Dale Elliman Balfour, 1963
Donna Rosenbaum Blaustein, 1964
Myrna Davidov, 1964
Clarinda Harriss Lott, 1960
Evelyn Dyke Schroedl, 1962

INTRODUCTION

A few introductory remarks about *The Pearl* are in order for the undergraduate and the general reader. These can be supplemented by referring to the volumes in the Selected Bibliography at the end of the volume.

The author is an unknown poet believed to have lived in the North-West Midlands of England in the second half of the fourteenth century. Thus, he was a contemporary of Geoffrey Chaucer. His dialect, however, since it is not the direct ancestor of modern English, presents greater difficulty to the twentieth-century reader than the London dialect in which Chaucer wrote. *The Pearl* exists in a single manuscript, which is on permanent display in the British Museum of London. This manuscript includes three other poems written in the same hand: *Sir Gawain and the Green Knight, Purity,* and *Patience.* On the evidence of dialect, vocabulary, and style, all four are usually (but not always) presumed to be the work of the same poet.

The form of the poem is four-stress alliterative lines, derived from the meter of much Anglo-Saxon poetry. To this pattern, the poet has added terminal rhymes, a complex design of *ababababbcbc,* in each of the twelve-line stanzas. There are 101 stanzas in the poem. Most critics believe that one stanza in group XV was to be omitted, though they do not agree on the specific stanza. The stanzas are divided into groups of five stanzas each, except for group XV, which has six stanzas. The *c* rhymes are the same throughout the five stanzas in each group, and the terminal lines of each stanza in a group repeat certain key words as well as the *same* rhyme word. The first line in the last four stanzas of each group contains a repeated word, as for example *spot* in group I, stanzas, 2, 3,

4, and 5. Moreover, each group, with the exception of XII, is linked to the next by a repetition from the terminal line of the preceding group in the initial line of the new group. Thus, *spot* in the last line of group I, stanza 5, "On þat prec[i]os perle wythouten *spot*" is the link to the first line of group II, stanza 1, "Fro *spot* my spyryt þer sprang in space." The final line of the poem (1212) "Ande precious perleʒ vnto his pay" links to line 1, "Perle plesaunte to prynces paye," which makes a perfect circle, or pearl, of the structure of the poem. This translation retains the technical structure of the poem in all its complexity.

There is wide divergence in the interpretation of *The Pearl*. The first editors and translators of the poem and, more recently, E. V. Gordon (1953) and A. C. Cawley (1962), as well as others, believe it to be an elegy on the death of a child, probably the poet's daughter. The first significant change in interpretation occurred in 1909, when W. H. Schofield presented the view that the pearl is a symbol of purity or virginity. In 1925, Sister Mary Madeleva interpreted the poem in a full-length book as *Pearl: A Study in Spiritual Dryness*. This view was supported by Sister Mary Vincent Hillman in her edition and literal translation of 1959 (although in 1945 in an article in *Modern Language Notes*, Sister Vincent had considered that the poem is about the loss of a literal pearl by a literal jeweler). The controversy between the two main theories is a lively one and numerous articles as well as editions and translations with notes have defended one or the other and continue to do so. But like Chase (1932) the present translators were "at no point forced to choose a phrase that was definitely incompatible with any one of the different interpretations." This version attempts to retain the ambiguities of the original and to leave the interpretation open.

The Pearl

I

1

Perle plesaunte to prynces paye
To clanly clos in golde so clere
Oute of Oryent I hardyly saye
Ne proued I neuer her precios pere
5 So rounde so reken in vche araye
So smal so smoþe her sydeȝ were
Quere so euer I jugged gemmeȝ gaye
I sette hyr sengely in synglure
Allas I leste hyr in on erbere
10 Þurȝ gresse to grounde hit fro me yot
I dewyne fordolked of luf daungere
Of þat pryuy perle wythouten spot

2

Syþen in þat spote hit fro me sprange
Ofte haf I wayted wyschande þat wele
15 Þat wont watȝ whyle deuoyde my wrange
& heuen my happe & al my hele
Þat dotȝ bot þrych my hert þrange
My breste in bale bot bolne & bele
Ȝet þoȝt me neuer so swete a sange
20 As stylle stounde let to me stele
For soþe þer fleten to me fele
To þenke hir color so clad in clot
O moul þou marreȝ a myry iuele
My priuy perle wythouten spotte

---

1 paye Literal translation would cause serious problem in complex rhyme scheme. **2 O** notes difficulty in interpretation of this line. Whether the gold is the coffer or the setting of a literal pearl, the translators prefer not to decide. Since the interpretation is highly controversial they have tried to translate in a way that does not prejudice any theory advanced thus far. **6 So smoþe her sydeȝ were** In the description of the pearl the translators wish to avoid any one interpretation. **9 erbere** O, *garden, lawn,* or *green.* See l. 38. **10 hit fro me yot** lit. *it went from me.* **11 luf-daungere** O, *love, bondage;* G, *I am pining away, grievously wounded, through the power of my love for my own pearl, that had no flaw.* **dewyne** H, past tense. The translators think it is present tense, because the state of grief continues. Loss of **dewyne** in NE makes *d* alliteration

I   1

Pearl, the precious prize of a king,
Chastely set in cherished gold,
In all the East none equalling,
No peer to her could I behold.
So round, so rare, a radiant thing,   5
So smooth she was, so small of mold,
Wherever I judged gems glimmering
I set her apart, her price untold.
Alas, I lost her in earth's green fold;
Through grass to the ground, I searched in vain.   10
I languish alone; my heart grows cold
For my precious pearl without a stain.

2

Since in that spot it slipped from me,
I lingered, longing for that delight
That from my sins once set me free   15
And my happiness raised to the highest height.
Her going wounds me grievously;
It burns my breast both day and night.
Yet I never imagined a melody
So sweet as she, so brief, and slight.   20
But memory flowed through my mind's sight:
I thought how her color in clods had lain,
O dust that dims what once was bright,
My precious pearl without a stain.

---

too difficult to follow. **12 spot** This word must be used for five stanzas. There are too few rhyme possibilities. In the terminal position *stain* has been substituted. **13 sprange** G, lit., *sprang*. **15 wrange** H, *sins*. May have a less theological connotation. **16 & heuen my happe & al me hele** *And raised up my good fortune and all my welfare.* **17 Þat dotȝ bot þrych my hert þrange** O, *that does pierce my heart constantly;* H, *afflict;* G, *grievously*. Repeated in other words in l. 18. The translators have varied the sense in l. 17. **18 bolne & bele** O, *swells and torments.* **19** O's and G's interpretation that the **swete . . . sange** is this poem, created in the stillness after the loss of the pearl, seems improbable. **22 color** O, *color;* G, *complexion;* H, *collar!* **23 O moul þou marreȝ a myry iuele** O *earth, thou marrest a lovely jewel.*

3

²⁵ Þat spot of spyseȝ [mo] t nedeȝ sprede
Þer such rycheȝ to rot is runne
Blomeȝ blayke & blwe & rede
Þer schyneȝ ful schyr agayn þe sunne
Flor & fryte may not be fede
³⁰ Þer hit doun drof in moldeȝ dunne
For vch gresse mot grow of grayneȝ dede
No whete were elleȝ to woneȝ wonne
Of goud vche goude is ay bygonne
So semly a sede moȝt fayly not
³⁵ Þat spryg ande spyceȝ vp ne sponne
Of þat precios perle wythouten spotte

4

To þat spot þat I in speche expoun
I entred in þat erber grene
In Auguste in a hyȝ seysoun
⁴⁰ Quen corne is coruen wyth crokeȝ kene
On huyle þer perle hit trendeled doun
Schadowed þis worteȝ ful schyre & schene
Gilofre gyngure & gromylyoun
& pyonys powdered ay bytwene
⁴⁵ Ȝif hit watȝ semly on to sene
A fayr reflayr ȝet fro hit flot
Þer wonys þat worþyly I wot & wene
My precious perle wythouten spot

---

25 Rare interpolated for metrical reasons. **29 fede** O, H, *withered?*
G, *faded*. **31 For vch gresse mot grow of grayneȝ dede** The grain
is not dead, in a scientific sense; it only appears to be. But that is
what the poet has said. John 12: 24-25 "Except a corn of wheat fall
into the ground and die, it abideth alone: but if it die, it bringeth
forth much fruit." **34 fayly** O, *fail*, in this context, surely *die;* G,
fail to be productive; H, *come to naught.* **35 spryg ande spyces**
H's emendation of G and O, **spry[n] gande spyceȝ up ne sponne**
that spices being born would not spring up. The translators prefer

3

Rare spices on that spot must spread: 25
Such riches there to rot have run,
Blooms of yellow and blue and red,
Their sheen a shimmer against the sun.
Flower and fruit nor faded nor dead,
Where the pearl dropped down in mouldering dun;   30
Each grass from a lifeless grain is bred,
Else to harvest no wheat were won:
Always from good is good begun.
So seemly a seed could not die in vain,
That sprig nor spice there would be none   35
Of that precious pearl without a stain.

4

To the spot which I in speech portray,
I entered in that arbor green,
In August on a holy day,
When the corn is cut with sickles keen.   40
On the little rise where my pearl rolled away,
The fairest flowers formed a screen:
Gillyflower, ginger, gromwell spray,
With peonies powdered in between.
If they were seemly to be seen,   45
Far sweeter the scents from that domain,
More worthy her dwelling, well I ween,
My precious pearl without a stain.

H's version to the interpolated [n] because the line thus is not re-
dundant. **37 in speche expoun** O, *declare, tell*; G, *describe*; H, *set
forth, describe*. Difficult to translate because it is an expletive but at
the same time an initial rhyme word. **38 erber** O, *grass, lawn* or
green; G, *grassy place in a garden, often among trees*; H, *garden*.
41 huyle O, G, *mound* or *bank*; H, *hillock*. **42** Lit., *these plants
shadowed*. There seems to be no obejct for this verb in the text.   **43**
gromwell Does it grow in sprays?

5

Bifore þat spot my honde I spenn[e]d
50 For care ful colde þat to me caȝt
A deuely dele in my hert denned
Þaȝ resoun sette myseluen saȝt
I playned my perle þat þer watȝ spenned
Wyth fyrte skylleȝ þat faste faȝt
55 Þaȝ kynde of Kryst me comfort kenned
My wreched wylle in wo ay wraȝte
I felle vpon þat floury flaȝt
Suche odour to my herneȝ schot
I slode vpon a slepyng-slaȝte
60 On þat prec[i]os perle wythouten spot

II   6

Fro spot my spyryt þer sprang in space
My body on balke þer bod in sweuen
My goste is gon in Godeȝ grace
In auenture þer meruayles meuen
65 I ne wyste in þis worlde quere þat hit wace
Bot I knew me keste þer klyfeȝ cleuen
Towarde a foreste I bere þe face
Where rych rokkeȝ wer to dyscreuen
Þe lyȝt of hem myȝt no mon leuen
70 Þe glemande glory þat of hem glent
For wern neuer webbeȝ þat wyȝeȝ weuen
Of half so dere adubmente

---

49 spenn[e]d O, G, *clasped;* H, *wrung, locked.* **51 O, A de[r]uely dele in my hert denned** *A sudden sorrow in my heart made tumult;* G, **deuely** *desolating, dreary;* **denned** *lurked deep,* H, *lodged.* Savage notes that **denned** may be derived from **dennan,** *resounded,* and the use of **playned** in l. 53 supports this idea. There is no necessary connection, however. **deuely** *devilish.* H interprets this as evil because it is contrary to reason and Christian teaching and is indulged in wilfully. Loss of **deruely (deuely)** made it difficult, if not impossible, to keep the *d*-alliteration of this line. The translators chose G's interpretation of **denned,** a verb lost in NE. H's interpretation, though it is probable, could not be included. **54 skylleȝ** O, G, H, *reasoning;* G, *With vehement thoughts that contended obstinately.* **55** Lit., *Though the nature of Christ imparted comfort to me.* The translators believe that ll. 55 and 56 mean that although comfort is to be found in the nature of Christ, and the dreamer knows this intellectually, he is unable to accept it emotionally. G's note is similar. **56** Hamilton and G point out that **wratȝe** is from the OE

5

I mourned, hands clenched, before that mound,
For the piercing cold of grief had caught   50
Me in the doleful dread and bound
My heart, though reason solace sought.
I longed for my pearl, locked in the ground,
While fierce contentions in me fought.
In Christ, though comfort could be found,   55
My wretched will was still distraught.
I fell upon that flowery plot.
Such odors eddied in my brain,
To sudden slumber I was brought
By that precious pearl without a stain.   60

II   6

From that spot my spirit sped through space,
While my body lay in earth-bound dream:
My spirit gone by God's sweet grace
Adventuring where visions stream.
I knew not in this world that place,   65
But I knew I was cast where cliffs a-beam
With richest rocks rose high to face
A forest. So splendid did they seem,
The light of them, the glorious gleam
None might believe—magnificent.   70
No mortal webs that men could seam
Had half so rare an ornament.

---

wrehrte meaning *was pained* or *suffered* (G), rather than from the OE **worchen,** as held by O, *wrought,* and Wright, *to strive.* **59 I slode vpon a slepyng-slazte** Loss of **slode** and **slazte** have damaged this line irreparably in translation. **61 in space** O, *space.* G's note disagrees; according to him, *after a time.* See *The Gret Hystoriale of the Destruction of Troy,* translated from *Historia Troiana* by Guido de Colonna (Early English Text Society), l. 2811. H says "**Space** in ME usually signifies an interval of time." Savage holds it is not *at once* but *after a while.* **65** Lit., *I did not know in this world where it was;* G, *I had no idea at all where it was.* **66 cleuen** O, *abide, stand fast;* G, H *clove the air, rose aloft,* past tense. *a-beam* necessitated by rhyme. **67** Ll. 67 and 68 have been transposed by the translators, and the face of the dreamer, **I bere þe face** has been put into verb form, so that the rocks face the forest, as the dreamer looks at them. **69** Ll. 69 and 70 again have been transposed in order to present the description with less inversion. **71** This change in metaphor is abrupt, but exact translation has required its inclusion. **72 adubmente** see note to l. 121.

7

Dubbed wern alle þo downeȝ sydeȝ
With crystal klyffeȝ so cler of kynde
75 Holte wodeȝ bryȝt aboute hem bydeȝ
Of bolleȝ as blwe as ble of ynde
As bornyst syluer þe lef onslydeȝ
Þat þike con trylle on vch a tynde
Quen glem of glodeȝ agaynȝ hem glydeȝ
80 Wyth schymeryng schene ful schrylle þay schynde
Þe grauayl þat on grounde con grynde
Wern precious perleȝ of Oryente
Þe sunnebemeȝ bot blo & blynde
In respecte of þat adubbement

8

85 The adubbements of þo downeȝ dere
Garten my goste al greffe forȝete
So frech flauoreȝ of fryteȝ were
As fode hit con me fayre refete
Fowleȝ þer flowen in fryth in fere
90 Of flaumbande hweȝ boþe smale & grete
Bot sytole-stryng & gyternere
Her reken myrþe moȝt not retrete
For quen þose bryddeȝ her wyngeȝ bete
Þay songen wyth a swete asent
95 So gracios gle couþe no mon gete
As here & se her adubbement

---

74 **of kynde** lit., *of nature*.   76 **ynde** O, G, *indigo blue*.   77 **onslydeȝ** O, *shift;* G, *slides on* (the trees). G says **on** *on them*, not **un** as held by O, Gollancz, and NED.   78 The translators believe that the intention was not to create a clatter of silver leaves in the wind, but to describe the sliding of the leaves against each other in the breeze, while the silver color shone in the light. This idea was derived from G's note, and from H.   79 **glodeȝ** NED, *bright place in the*

7

The downs were adorned on every side
With crystal cliffs that clearly show;
Forests bright about them abide,   75
The tree boles the blue of indigo.
Like burnished silver the bright leaves slide,
Thick branches a-quiver when breezes blow,
And gleams of sunlight against them glide,
With a shimmering sheen their splendors glow.   80
The gravel I ground where my steps would go
Was precious pearls of the Orient;
The sunbeams were dark as the depths below
Compared to so rare an ornament.

8

In seeing those downs adorned so fair,   85
My spirit forgot its suffering.
The fragrance of fruit so fresh and rare,
Like food, was fully nourishing;
Flocks of birds were flying there,
Both small and great, flamed, glistening,   90
In reckless mirth. That marvelous air
No one could sound on cithole string,
For when those birds rose, wing to wing,
They sang so sweetly in concent.
Such gracious mirth no man could bring   95
As the sound, the sight of this ornament.

---

sky, flash of light; also, O, H, G, *clear patches of sky.* Origins obscure. **83 blo & blynde** O, G, lit., *dark and dim.* **91-92** These lines were transposed by the translators to deal more effectively with rhyme and meter. **93 her wyngeȝ bete** O, H, lit., *beat their wings;* G, *flew.* **95** Lit., *no man could sing a sight,* but the poet has **coupe no mon gete / As here & se her adubbement.** To use *glee* would produce unfortunate connotations.

9

So al watȝ dubbet on dere asyse
Þat fryth þer fortwne forth me fereȝ
Þe derþe þerof for to deuyse
100 Nys no wyȝ worþe þat tonge bereȝ
I welke ay forth in wely wyse
No bonk so byg þat did me dereȝ
Þe fyrre in þe fryth þe fei[r]er con ryse
Þe playn þe plottteȝ þe spyse þe pereȝ
105 & raweȝ & randeȝ & rych reuereȝ
As fyldor fyn her b[o]nkes brent
I wan to a water by schore þat schereȝ
Lorde dere watȝ hit adubbement

10

The dubbemente of þo derworth depe
110 Wern bonkeȝ bene of beryl bryȝt
Swangeande swete þe water con swepe
Wyth a rownande rourde raykande aryȝt
In þe founce þer stonden stoneȝ stepe
As glente þurȝ glas þat glowed & glyȝt
115 A[s] stremande sterneȝ quen stroþe-men slepe
Staren in welkyn in wynter nyȝt
For vche a pobbel in pole þer pyȝt
Watȝ emerad saffer oþer gemme gente
Þat all þe loȝe lemed of lyȝt
120 So dere watȝ hit adubbement

---

97 asyse O, *manner;* G, *fashion;* H, *fashion, manner.* **102 No bonk so byg þat did me dereȝ** Lit., *no bank so big that did me harm, or annoyance.* **dereȝ** G, *hindrance;* H, verb, *to hinder,* or *trouble.* **104 pereȝ** lit., *pears.* Ludicrous with *plain, plants, spices.* The translators left it out. The poet needed it for his rhyme. **106** The translators think that this was a description of the bank, where it meets the water, seen as a fine gold line or thread. See also ll. 165 and 166 where a similar interpretation and translation is made. O thinks the bank is embroidered with leaves and flowers. G remarks that a bank in ME is a feature of the ground, not the water but the place where the land meets the stream. H has no comment. **107 schereȝ** O, lit., *run swiftly by;* G, *meanders along,* with a long note on possible origin and meaning; H, *swerves, winds.* Translation is altered for

9

So all was adorned in dearest guise,
That forest that Fortune led me to.
Its excellence to eulogize,
To tell its worth, no tongue speaks true.   100
But still I walked in blissful wise;
No barrier barred my journey through.
The farther I went, the fairer did rise
The plants, the herbs, and the plain to view,
Hedgerows and borders, broad rivers, too,   105
Their banks like fine gold filament.
To the water's edge I went and knew,
O Lord, how lovely that ornament.

10

The adornment of that dear-loved deep
Was beautiful banks of beryl bright;   110
The whirling water did softly sweep,
A murmurous river running aright.
In the depths the stones their sparkle keep,
As if through glass. They glow as white
As streaming stars when mortals sleep   115
Shine in the welkin a winter night.
Set in the pool, the pebbles in sight
Were emerald, sapphire—stones that lent
To all the pool a living light,
So dear was all that ornament.   120

rhyme. **109 derworth** O, *rare;* G, *splendid;* H, *precious.* Word is
lost and difficult to replace in translation. From **der** *dear,* and **worth**
valuable, the translators derived *dear-loved.* **111 swangeande** O,
rush?; G, *swirling;* H, *swinging, moving rhythmically;* Emerson,
swange + **ande,** hence *slender, slim, graceful,* hence *pretty* or *pleas-*
ant. There is no break in MS between **swange** and **ande. 115 strope**
O suggests *hidden, close, secure,* rather than *bold, fierce;* G, *men of*
this earth; he notes that the word is of uncertain derivation, but
gives it this "generalized poetic sense," and says it "would probably
carry with it also, pictorially, a suggestion of dark, low earth onto
which the high stars look down." Derived from ON **stord** *stalks of*
herbage; H, *mortals.* H quotes G and Onion's *growth-covered earth,*
from Icelandic poetry.

III   11

The dubbement dere of doun & daleȝ
Of wod & water & wlonk playneȝ
Bylde in me blys abated my baleȝ
Fordidden my stresse dystryed my payneȝ
125 Doun after a strem þat dryȝly haleȝ
I bowed in blys bredful my brayneȝ
Þe fyrre I folȝed þose floty valeȝ
Þe more strenghþe of ioye myn herte strayneȝ
As Fortune fares þer as ho frayneȝ
130 Wheþer solace ho sende oþer elleȝ sore
Þe wyȝ to wham her wylle ho wayneȝ
Hytteȝ to haue ay more & more

12

More of wele watȝ in þat wyse
Þen I cowþe telle þaȝ I tom hade
135 For vrþely herte myȝt not suffyse
To þe tenþe dole of þo gladneȝ glade
Forþy I þoȝte þat Paradyse
Watȝ þer oþer gayn þo bonkeȝ brade
I hoped þe water were a deuyse
140 Bytwene myrþeȝ by mereȝ made
Byȝonde þe broke by slente oþer slade
I hope þat mote merked wore
Bot þe water watȝ depe I dorst not wade
& euer me longed a more & more

121 **dubbement** O, *array, splendor*; G, H, *adornment*. Because of its
key position in the final lines of stanzas 6 to 11 and the opening
lines of stanzas 7 to 11, translation of this word was extremely
difficult. 129-132 O gives no note, except that the poet's attitude
towards Fortune is more patient and sane than is usual for his time.
G, "*Even as fortune acts wherever she makes trial, whether she
allot delight or sorrow, the man to whom she sends her will chances
(in result) to have ever more and more;* Fortune visits whatever man
she wishes to test, sending him continuous good or bad luck for the
time being. The idea of Fortune as a fickle goddess testing the hearts
of men was common in mediaeval literature." H chooses *is likely*
from L. **periculo se exponere.** "This meaning would seem more suit-
able here than that proposed by OED—'aim, seek, strive,' since
the recipient of '*sore*,' '*sorrow*,' from Fortune would scarcely seek,
strive for, or aim at more." The translators solved the problems in
ll. 131 and 132 by indicating that the man who realizes that he
is on the upward turn of Fortune's wheel will have more and more
good Fortune, and that the converse is true, though both good and

III   11

The dear adornment of down and dale,
Of wood and water and wondrous plain,
Enhanced my bliss, beguiled my bale,
Put by my distress, destroyed my pain.
By the flowing currents which never fail,   125
I bowed while bliss imbued my brain.
The farther I followed this flowery vale
The stronger did joy my heart sustain.
Though Fortune fares where she may deign,
To send us solace or trial sore,   130
Who tokens of her will attain
Shall come to have still more and more.

12

More beauty was there beyond all price
Than I could tell, though time were stayed,
For mortal heart might not suffice   135
To feel a tenth of that joy displayed.
Therefore I thought that Paradise
Beyond that bank must be arrayed;
I hoped that the water was mere device
'Twixt joy and joy, a boundary laid.   140
Beyond the brook, by slope or glade,
I hoped to see a city soar,
But the water was deep, and I dared not wade,
And ever I longed still more and more.

bad Fortune come to an end as the wheel turns. **Hytteȝ** O, *aim, strive;* G, *chances, attains as a result;* H, *is likely, runs the chance.* **133 wele** O, G, H, *joy.* 136 **gladneȝ** O refers to a note, but there is none; G, *joys;* H, *gladness;* Emerson, plural of **gladen** *open space* or *glade.* The alliteration on *g* has been lost in the translation. **139 hope** H, *guessed, surmised;* O, "not with modern meaning." **140 By-twene myrþeȝ by mereȝ made** lit., *Between joys, by the waters made.* O has *boundary* for **mereȝ.** The translators thought the river is a boundary between the joys of earth and those of heaven, a sense suggested by G's note, though this interpretation is not his. G gives *pool* for **mereȝ.** H also has *boundaries* and a note suggesting that these exist in heaven between various states of beatitude. **142 merked** H, *reached;* O, *placed;* G, *situated.* The translators, on the evidence later in the poem and in Revelation, think that there must be a city there, though the dreamer only thinks so, since he has not yet seen it, and also that he hopes to cross the river to reach it. L1. 142 and 143 together in the translation try to suggest both ideas. Savage has **merked** *lay out.*

13

145 More & more & ʒet wel mare
Me lyste to se þe broke byʒonde
For if hit watʒ fayr þer I con fare
Wel loueloker watʒ þe fyrre londe
Abowte me con I stote & stare
150 To fynde a forþe faste con I fonde
Bot woþeʒ mo iwysse þer ware
Þe fyrre I stalked by þe stronde
& euer me þoʒt I schulde not wonde
For wo þer weleʒ so wynne wore
155 Þenne nwe note me com on honde
Þat meued my mynde ay more & more

14

More meruayle con my dom adaunt
I seʒ byʒonde þat myry mere
A crystal clyffe ful relusaunt
160 Mony ryal ray con fro hit rere
At þe fote þerof þer sete a faunt
A mayden of menske ful debonere
Blysnande whyt watʒ hyr bleaunt
I knew hyr wel I hade sen hyr ere
165 As glysnande golde þat man con schere
So schon þat schene anvnder schore
On lenghe I loked to hyr þere
Þe lenger I knew hyr more & more

---

147 *fair*-and-*fare* play is in the original.   149 Lit., *About me could I stop and stare.*   150 H, *To find a ford quickly did I try.*   151 woþeʒ O, *dangers;* G, *perils;* H, *hunts, searchings.*   154 *For woe, where joys so blessed* or *so easy to win;* O and H give wynne in both meanings; G prefers *delightful, precious.*   155 on honde Savage, *speedily;* O, *came to my notice;* G, *became evident;* H, *to my attention came.*   159 reluçent literal translation, but word unusual in NE.   161 faunt in sense of *young person,* lost in NE. Translation is rather archaic, therefore not entirely accurate. Savage suggests *a high-born or aristocratic appearing child.*   163 designed

13

More and more, while I waited there,   145
I yearned to see beyond the strand,
For if it was fair where I could fare,
Far lovelier was the farther land.
There I stopped to consider where
I could find a crossing, a ford that spanned.   150
Of other dangers I was aware
The farther I strolled along the sand,
And always it seemed I should not stand
In woe, when weal lay all before.
Then a novel wonder drew near to hand   155
Which moved my mind still more and more.

14

More marvels were there to daunt my mind:
I saw beyond that stream so fair
A crystal cliff relucent shined
And royal rays rose into air.   160
Below the cliff a maid reclined,
A damsel of mien all debonaire,
Her dress in dazzling white designed.
I knew her well; I had seen her ere.
Like glistening gold men carve with care   165
Shimmered the light along that shore;
I looked at her a long while there—
Knowing, I knew her more and more.

rhyme word. **165 As glysnande golde þat man con schere** O, *gold cut into fine threads;* G, **schere,** *to make bright or pure* (l. 213 **schorne gold** *has been cut*) **166 So schon þat schene anvnder schore** G, *cut* into strips to make **fyldor** *gold threads, the girl's hair.* **schore** H, *hill;* O, G, *cliffs above the bank;* but elsewhere all three translate it as *shore, bank.* The translators think here, not of the maiden nor of her hair, but of the gold thread of light running along the bank of a river where the water meets the shore, as in 1. 165 above.

15 *

The more I frayste hyr fayre face
170 Her fygure fyn quen I had fonte
Suche gladande glory con to me glace
As lyttel byfore þerto watȝ wonte
To calle hyr lyste con me enchace
Bot baysment gef myn hert a brunt
175 I seȝ hyr in so strange a place
Such a burre myȝt make myn herte blunt
Þenne vereȝ ho vp her fayre frount
Hyr vysayge whyt as playn yuore
Þat stonge myn hert ful stray atount
180 & euer þe lenger þe more & more

IV   16

More þen me lyste my drede aros
I stod ful stylle & dorste not calle
Wyth yȝen open & mouth ful clos
I stod as hende as hawk in halle
185 I hope þat gostly watȝ þat porpose
I dred onende quat schulde byfalle
Lest ho me eschaped þat I þer chos
Er I at steuen hir moȝt stalle
Þat gracios gay wythouten galle
190 So smoþe so smal so seme slyȝt
Ryseȝ vp in hir araye ryalle
A precios pyece in perleȝ pyȝt

---

* In spite of O's enthusiastic note aboute the beauty of stanzas 15
and 16, they are extremely difficult to translate, especially stanza 15.
which seemed to the translators repetitive and full of padding.

172 G, *As had hitherto been wont* (*to come*). **174 gef myn hert a
brunt** O, G, H, *gave my heart a blow*. **baysment** O, *confusion of
mind;* G, *confusion due to surprise;* H, *amazement.* The translators
think H's interpretation is more appropriate to the rest of the
stanza. **179 stray** O, *out of the straight course;* G, *in bewilder-*

15 *

The more I gazed on her fair face,
Her figure fine, the more I found   170
Such gladdening glory that came apace
As seldom before did so abound.
Desire to call her did embrace
My heart; amazement stilled the sound.
To see her in so strange a place,   175
The blow so sudden did astound.
She raised her face, her forehead crowned
In ivory white; her visage bore
A beauty that could my sense confound,
And ever the longer, more and more.   180

IV   16

Far more than I liked my fear arose.
I stood quite still and dared not call.
Mute and watchful in wonder's throes,
Gentle I stood as a hawk in hall,
And mystic meaning did suppose. \   185
I believed, yet feared, what should befall,
Lest she should vanish before I chose,
Before, by speaking, I might forestall
That gracious gay one virginal,
So smooth, so small, so seemly slight,   190
She rose in robes imperial,
A precious vision in pearls bedight.

ment; H, *distractedly, to distraction.* Lit., *That stung my heart, con-
founded out of the straight course;* G, *Which threw my heart into
astounded confusion.* **183** Not in the original but **yȝen open &
mouth ful clos** indicates it. **184 hende** *tame?* **185** Using *purpose*
would present a problem in rhyme and stress—*I hope that the in-
tent/purpose was spiritual.* **187 chos** O, G, *discerned?* **189** run-
on; O, a period after **stalle**; H, G, a comma. **191 ryalle** sense dis-
torted slightly for the rhyme. **192 pyece** *person.* Pejoration has
occurred; some substitution is required.

17

Perleȝ pyȝte of ryal prys
Þere moȝt mon by grace haf sene
195 Quen þat frech as flor-de-lys
Doun þe bonke con boȝe bydene
Al blysnande whyt watȝ hir beaumys
Vpon at sydeȝ & bounden bene
Wyth þe myryeste margarys at my deuyse
200 Þat euer I seȝ ȝet with myn yȝen
Wyth lappeȝ large I wot & I wene
Dubbed with double perle & dyȝte
Her cortel of self sute schene
Wyth precios perleȝ al vmbepyȝte

18

205 A pyȝt coroune ȝet wer þat gyrle
Of mariorys & non oþer ston
Hiȝe pynakled of cler quyt perle
Wyth flurted flowereȝ perfet vpon
To hed hade ho non oþer werle
210 Her lere leke al hyr vmbe gon
Her semblaunt sade for doc oþer erle
Her ble more blaȝt þen whalleȝ bon
As schorne golde schyr her fax þenne schon
On schyldereȝ þat leghe vnlapped lyȝte
215 Her depe colour ȝet wonted non
Of precios perle in porfyl pyȝte

196 H, *came forthwith down the bank.* **197** *fleece* not in original.
G says MS Apocalypse 19:8, bride of the Lamb was allowed *to
array herself in shining white bysse.* G amends to **beau biys** *fair
linen;* H to **beaumys** *mantle* or *surcoat.* **200** Lit., *That ever yet I
saw with my eyes.* Loss of **yȝen** makes it necessary to rearrange the
rhymes. **201 lappeȝ** O, *loose folds;* G, *hanging sleeves;* H, *lappets,
folds.* **206 mariorys** O, *pearl.* **margarita** in L. means *pearl.* Loss of
this meaning in NE severely limits variations in the vocabulary used
to describe the pearl. **209** Lit., *on her head she had no other fillets.*
Ll. 209 and 210 are reversed. **210** O, [h]ere-leke *locks of hair;* G,
here-leke, G says **leke** *enclosed.* H and Hamilton, **lere-leke** *face
radiance.* Cawley gives *wimple,* an idea with which Hamilton agrees.
The translation is disputed. O, *Her locks of hair encircle her;* G, *Her
hair lying all about her, enclosed her countenance;* H, *Her face*

17

Of royal pearls a precious piece
There might men by grace have seen,
Where she as fresh as fleur-de-lys   195
Came stepping down the sloping green;
Her gown was glistening white like fleece,
With open sides, all bound between
By perfect pearls. I could not cease
To stare at their unequalled sheen,   200
Her robe with fullest folds, I ween,
Adorned with double pearls, all bright.
Her kirtle, styled the same, serene
With precious pearls was all bedight.

18

That maiden wore a costly whorl   205
Of marguerites, no other stone,
In pinnacles of pure white pearl
And figured flowers perfectly sewn,
Around her face a radiant swirl,
Crowned with the circlet, this crown alone.   210
Her semblance solemn as duke or earl,
Her color was whiter than white whale bone.
Like carven gold her curls there shone,
Lay on her shoulders, loose and light;
Her pure complexion bore the tone   215
Of pearls embroidered and bedight.

radiance shining all about her. The problem of textual emendation
is too complicated for the translators, but they are not convinced by
H's argument that the description proceeds in an orderly way—the
crown would logically be followed by hair. Actually the text describes
hair, face, and complexion in ll. 213, 211, 212, and 215, in that
order. The translators have used *radiant swirl*, which may be either
face-radiance or *hair*. They understand that the maiden wears only
one crown, but see no objection to two descriptions of her hair and
her complexion in the same stanza, since the descriptions apparently
do not contradict each other. **215-216 colour** O, *color of skin;* G,
complexion; H, *collar.* G's translation, *The deep white of her com-
plexion lacked nothing of the color of the precious pearls set in
the embroidery,* seems reasonable.

19

Pyȝt watȝ poyned & vche a hemme
At honde at sydeȝ at ouerture
Wyth whyte perle & non oþer gemme
220 & bornyste quyte watȝ hyr uesture
Bot a wonder perle wythouten wemme
In myddeȝ hyr breste watȝ sette so sure
A manneȝ dom moȝt dryȝly demme
Er mynde moȝt malte in hit mesure
225 I hope no tong moȝt endure
No sauerly saghe say of þat syȝt
So watȝ hit clene & cler & pure
Þat precios perle þer hit watȝ pyȝt

20 *

Pyȝt in perle þat precios pyce
230 On wyþer half water com doun þe schore
No gladder gome heþen into Grece
Þen I quen ho on brymme wore
Ho watȝ me nerre þen aunte or nece
My joy forþy watȝ much þe more
235 Ho p[ro]fered me speche þat special spece
Enclynande lowe in wommon lore
Caȝte of her coroun of grete tresore
& haylsed me wyth a lote lyȝte
Wel watȝ me þat euer I watȝ bore
240 To sware þat swete in perleȝ pyȝte

---

217 MS, **Pyȝt watȝ poyned** *adorned, cuffed*. **218 ouerture** O, G, *opening*. In this sense, lost in NE and therefore presenting a serious problem in translation and rhyme. **220 bornyste quyte** lit., *burnished white;* O, *lustrous;* G, *shining;* H, *lustrous*. **221** O has a long note on the symbolic significance of the pearl set on the maiden's bosom. **225-226** G, *I believe no tongue could suffice to say any adequate word of that sight.* G has a long note on mediaeval costume, with some reference to the symbolic significance of the pearls, as found in the Bible and in mediaeval lapidaries.

* In stanza 20 the translators believe that both "niece" and "Greece" are necessitated by rhyme, although they recognize the difficulty in interpretation presented by l. 233 **Ho watȝ me nerre þen aunte or nece.**

19

Beaded and bordered every hem,
At the wrists, the sides, each aperture,
With white pearls and no other gem,
Her dress was dazzling white, demure.   220
A faultless pearl no flaws condemn
Upon her breast was set secure.
The human mind must all thought stem
Before it judge this gem's allure.
I know no tongue that could endure   225
To tell the sweetness of that sight,
So clean it was and clear and pure,
That precious pearl that was bedight.

20 *

Bedight in pearl that masterpiece,
Across the stream, came toward the shore.   230
No gladder man from here to Greece
Than I when I saw her stand before
Me, nearer to me than aunt or niece,
So that my joy was much the more.
She began to speak and, in sweet release   235
Of womanly grace, the crown she wore
She removed, the wreath of richest ore,
And greeted me gaily, her manner bright.
Blest was my birth that I could adore
And speak to that sweet in pearls bedight.   240

229 pyce in MS, O & H, **py[ec]e;** G, **p[ec]e.** See note to l. 192.   **232** Loss of the form **wore** for *was* necessitates a change in the translation.   **235 p[ro]fered** in MS. The translators believe that she did not actually speak, but indicated that she wished to speak, since, at this point, no words are spoken nor message given. O thinks **spece** usually spelled **spyce;** G, *person;* H, *being.* O believes the word to be *spice,* in the sense that the Virgin is spoken of as **spice swettist of savior,** Early English Text Society 24.5.29, and 47n.   **237** It is not clear why she removed her crown before beginning to speak.   **238 lote lyȝte** O, *blithe manner;* G, *glad speech;* H, *cheerful word.*   **240 To sware** O, G, H, lit., *to answer.*

V   21

O perle quod I in perleȝ pyȝt
Art þou my perle þat I haf playned
Regretted by myn one on nyȝte
Much longeyng haf I for þe layned
245 Syþen into gresse þou me aglyȝte
Pensyf payred I am forpayned
& þou in a lyf of lykyng lyȝte
In paradys erde of stryf vnstrayned
What wyrde hatȝ hyder my iuel vayned
250 & don me in þys del & gret daunger
Fro we in twynne wern towen & twayned
I haf ben a joyleȝ juelere

22

That juel þenne in gemmeȝ gente
Vered vp her vyse wyth yȝen graye
255 Set on hyr coroun of perle orient
& soberly after þenne con ho say
Sir ȝe haf your tale myse tente
To say your perle is al awaye
Þat is in cofer so comly clente
260 As in þis gardyn gracios gaye
Hereinne to lenge for euer & play
Þer mys nee mornyng com neuer here
Her were a forser for þe in faye
If þou were a gentyl jueler

---

242 playned H, lit., *mourned;* the problem of finding six rhymes for
this, however, proved too difficult, hence the resort to archaism. G
does not include it in his glossary. **244 layned** O, *keep silent about;*
G, H, *concealed.* **245** H translates **aglyȝte** as *glittered away.* This
is suggested by the derivations supplied in O's glossary but not in
that of G. **247** This line sounds ineffective in NE but it is trans-
lated literally. **249 vayned** O, *brought;* H, *fetched, brought;* G, *sent.*
250 *pain's prisoner* a very free rendering of **þys del & gret daunger;**
O, *wailing and great bondage;* G, *grief and great distress;* H, *grief
and great power, danger, duress.* **253** *dressed* added to the literal
translation for sake of rhyme. **256-258** These lines have been run
on for smoother translation. *taken* is not literally in text. **soberly** O,
G, *gravely;* H, *seriously.* The mixture of *you* and *thou* forms in this
stanza also occurs in the text. **259-260 clente** not in O glossary; H,

V   21

"O Pearl," quoth I, "in pearls bedight,
Art thou my pearl that I have plained,
Longed for all alone by night?
With silent grief my heart ingrained,
Since, glittering in the grass, thy flight   245
Left me pensive, worn and pained,
And thou in a life of pleasure light
In Paradise, by strife unstrained.
What fate has there my fair detained
And left me to be pain's prisoner?   250
We, once together, were torn, constrained,
Till I was a joyless jeweler."

22

That jewel then in fair gems dressed
Gazed at me with her eyes of gray;
Placed her crown of pearl at rest   255
Upon her head and paused to say
Soberly, "Sir, you have wrongly expressed
Your tale that your pearl was taken away,
That is in so choice a treasure chest
As is this garden gracious, gay,   260
Herein to dwell forever and play
Where loss nor mourning never were.
Here were a coffer for thee, in fay,
If thou wert a gentle jeweler.

secured; G, *riveted, fastened.* G suggests alternative translations:
*which is in a coffer so fairly riveted, being in this garden so charm-
ingly gay;* or *Your pearl . . . which is enclosed in coffer so fairly
as to be in this garden.* **261** There is no alliteration in this line in
text or translation. **262** H, **here;** O, [n]**ere;** G, **nere;** O and G, **nere.**
Does this mean that G is emending the MS as he says in his "Note
on the Edited Text" "for corrections or scribal errors"? There is no
specific note in G on this line and square brackets are not used in
text. H's note says it is **here** in the MS and attributes G's and O's
change to punctuation (O has a semi-colon; G, a period). H also
has a period. H's translation: *Since neither loss nor mourning exists
here in Heaven, here indeed would be your true treasure chest.* "The
second **here** is pleonastic." The MS is nearly illegible but it appears
to be **nere.**

23

265 Bot jueler gente if þou schal lose
Þy ioy for a gemme þat þe watȝ lef
Me þynk þe put in a mad porpose
& busyeȝ þe aboute a raysoun bref
For þat þou lesteȝ watȝ bot a rose
270 Þat flowred & fayled as kynde hyt gef
Now þurȝ kynde of þe kyste þat hyt con close
To a perle of prys hit is put in pref
& þou hatȝ called þy wyrde a þef
Þat oȝt of noȝt hatȝ mad þe cler
275 Þou blameȝ þe bote of þy meschef
Þou art no kynde jueler

24

A juel to me þen watȝ þys geste
& iueleȝ wern hyr gentyl saweȝ
Iwyse quod I my blysfol beste
280 My grete dystresse þou al todraweȝ
To be excused I make requeste
I trawed my perle don out of daweȝ
Now haf I fonde hyt I schal ma feste
& wony wyth hyt in schyr wod-schaweȝ
285 & loue my Lorde & al his laweȝ
Þat hatȝ me broȝ þys blys ner
Now were I at yow byȝonde þise waweȝ
I were a ioyfol jueler

---

268 raysoun bref lit.. *temporary (transient) consideration;* G, *ground,
cause;* H, *cause.* **271-272** Coincidentally, these lines are almost ex-
actly Chase's translation. This and the following line appear to
mean that the nature of the coffer that held the pearl shows the
true value of the pearl. If the coffer is taken to be the human body
and the pearl the spirit, the meaning is quite difficult. If the coffer
represents God, or Heaven, where the pearl is now, while the
dreamer mistakenly supposed the coffer to be the body, then the
present abode of the pearl does show the true value. **pref** O, *proof;*
G, *has proved in fact to be;* H, *test.* **274** Lit., *aught from naught*
but the dreamer has supposed the loss of the pearl to be *naught.*
Properly understood, he has gained *aught* from the loss, or *naught,*
though he calls this happening or destiny a "thief" who stole his
pearl from him and calls the loss a deprivation when it is actually
the remedy or means of his salvation. O's notes indicate, but do not
clarify, the difficulties implicit in this line. G, like O, believes that

23

"But gentle jeweler, if joy goes   265
With the loss of a gem that was loved by thee,
Thou dost waste thyself in worthless woes,
Busied by such brief transiency.
What thou hast lost was but a rose
That flowered and failed most naturally: 270
The coffer that doth thy pearl enclose
Hath proved it a priceless pearl to be.
A thief thou hast dubbed thy destiny,
When naught from aught thou didst infer,
And wrongly thou blamest the remedy: 275
Thou art no natural jeweler."

24

A jewel to me was this guest,
And jeweled was each gentle phrase.
"Truly," said I, "my blissful best,
My great distress thy speech allays.   280
To be excused I make request:
I believed my pearl gone from my gaze.
Now I have found it, I feast, and, blest,
Shall dwell with it in woodland ways
And love my Lord and His laws praise.   285
Such bliss this blessing did confer
That were I beyond this water's maze
With you, I were joyful jeweler."

the pearl has been made from a rose. Both commentators have
confused two metaphors. The *Pearl*-poet separates them distinctly.
H has three long notes on these lines; she assumes that the coffer
is earth and of no value, but this reading is exactly the reverse of
what the lines say, although she is correct in thinking that the loss
of the pearl will lead the dreamer to a knowledge of true value. In
orthodox theology, the belief that the natural world was created by
God from naught is accepted; that He created it from *aught* or
chaos is heresy. **276** Alliteration on soft *g* has been lost in trans-
lation. **282-284 daweȝ** G, *put out of the world, dead;* H, *utterly
gone;* lit., *put out of days.* **ma feste** probably *to make a festival.*
The translators consider here the sight of her a feast for the eyes.
H, *make merry;* G, *rejoice;* Savage, *make fast,* that is, *not to let her
get away.* **schyr** *bright,* lost in translation. **286 ner** *near.* The prob-
lem of rhyming with the repeated *jeweler* of this grouping is great.

25 *

Jueler sayde þat gemme clene
290 Wy borde ȝe men so madde ȝe be
Þre wordeȝ hatȝ þou spoken at ene
Vnavysed forsoþe wern alle þre
Þou ne woste in worlde quat on dotȝ mene
Þy worde byfore þy wytte con fle
295 Þou says þou traweȝ me in þis dene
Bycawse þou may wyth yȝen me se
Anoþer þou says in þys countre
Þyself schal won wyth me ryȝt here
Þe þrydde to passe þys water fre
300 Þat may no ioyfol jueler

VI   26

I halde þat iueler lyttel to prayse
Þat loueȝ wel þat he seȝ wyth yȝe
& much to blame & vncortoyse
Þat leueȝ oure Lorde wolde make a lyȝe
305 Þat lelly hyȝte your lyf to rayse
Þaȝ fortune dyd your flesch to dyȝe
Ȝe setten hys wordeȝ ful westernays
Þat leueȝ noþynk bot ȝe hit syȝe
& þat is a poynt o sorquydryȝe
310 Þat vche god mon may euel byseme
To leue no tale be true to tryȝe
Bot þat hys one skyl may dem

---

* In this stanza, as in others, the use of the *thee* and *thou* form is consistent with the original; we have tried to keep it so in the text.

291 wordeȝ lit., *words* but actually *statements*. This usage is noted in "The seven last words of Christ." **at ene** *at once*. The word is lost, and the whole rhyming series must be altered. **292** Assonance rather than alliteration is used in the translation. **293** H translates lit., *Thou knowest not what on earth one doth mean*. Alliteration on *w* has been lost in this translation. **294** Translation is literal. Meaning is less clear; the dreamer is speaking without thinking. **298**

25 *

"Jeweler," said that gem so fair,
"Why mock, ye men, so mad ye be?   290
At once three words thou didst declare,
And ill-advised, in truth, all three;
Of any meaning unaware,
Thy words before thy wits must flee:
To deem me in this vale, to dare   295
To trust thine eyes which seem to see;
Further, thou seekst to stay with me
Within this place—again you err;
The third, to cross this water free,
As may no joyful jeweler.   300

VI   26

"I give that jeweler little praise
Who values what he views with eye,
And much to blame and base the ways
Of him who thinks our Lord would lie.
In faith He swore your soul to raise,   305
Though Fortune caused your flesh to die—
You make His words a worthless phrase,
Believing what you can espy,
And such presumption I decry
In worthy men. It would ill beseem   310
To trust no tale and to rely
Only on what your judgments deem.

---

again you err is not in text. Added to fill out rhyme. **302 louez** clearly in MS; G, **leuez; H, [ce]uez wyth yze** *with eye.* **303 vncortoyse** O, *ungracious;* G, H, *discourteous.* Translation altered for sake of rhyme. **305 lelly** O, G, H, *faithfully.* **307 esternays, [b]esternays** O, *awry;* **westernays** G, *reversed, awry.* G says *b & w* closely similar in many mediaeval hands; H, nothing in glossary. See H in *Modern Language Notes,* LVIII, p. 42 **westernays** *empty pledge;* therefore, *You account His words a quite empty pledge who . . . believe nothing unless you see it.* **312 skyl** O, G, H, *judgment, reason.*

27

Deme now þyself if þou con dayly
As man to God wordeȝ schulde heue
315 Þou saytȝ þou schal won in þis bayly
Me þynk þe burde fyrst aske leue
& ȝet of graunt þou myȝteȝ fayle
Þou wylneȝ ouer þys water to weue
Er moste þou ceuer to oþer counsayl
320 Þy corse in clot mot calder keue
For hit watȝ forgarte at paradys greue
Oure ȝore fader hit con mysseȝeme
Þurȝ drwry deth boȝ vch ma dreue
Er ouer þys dam hym dryȝtyn deme

28

325 Demeȝ þou me quod I my swete
To dol agayn þenne I dowyne
Now haf I fonte þat I forlete
Schal I efte forgo hit er euer I fyne
Why shal I hit boþe mysse & mete
330 My precios perle dotȝ me gret pyne
What serueȝ tresor bot gareȝ men grete
When he hit schal efte wyth teneȝ tyne
Now rech I neuer for to declyne
Ne how fer of folde þat man me fleme
335 When I am partleȝ of perleȝ myne
Bot durande doel what may men deme

313-314 O, *Judge now thyself whether thou didst speak idly according to the words which man ought to offer to God* **dayly** O, *idly;* H, *speak idly;* G, *contend, dispute* and note on confusion of spellings and meanings in MS. Savage refers to Emerson's **dayly** *complain, contend. deem* is used throughout these stanzas as a link word, both at the beginning and the end of each. In NE it has a distractingly archaic sound; for this reason the translators have not used it consistently. **to God wordeȝ shulde heue** Literal translation is ludicrous. The *b* rhyme of *God* was adopted reluctantly after attempts with *high* and *try*. **316** Lit., *it behooves thee first to ask leave.* **317** O and G end this line with a period; the translators have run on. There is no punctuation in MS. **319 ceuer** *attain.* The translators have achieved the intention, but not the literal translation

27

"Deem thyself if idly thou,
Like a man who rashly rails at God,
Sayst this dwelling shalt be thine now.   315
First thou shouldst seek to see the nod
Of granting, yet still mayst fail somehow
To cross this stream. Accept the rod,
A plan which passage would allow:
Thy flesh must lie in coldest clod,   320
Since it was stricken on Eden's sod.
Our forefather did it misesteem:
Through dreary death each man must plod,
Ere God doom him beyond this stream."

28

"My sweet," quoth I, "doomest thou me   325
To dolor again, to deep decline?
What I lamented at last I see;
Before I die must I thee resign?
Must I both miss and meet with thee,
My precious pearl for which I pine?   330
What is treasure but torment when we
Again to grieving must incline?
Now I never care how I repine,
Nor how men force me to the extreme,
When parted from that pearl of mine,   335
Save enduring grief what may men deem?"

here. **320 keue** H, *sink;* O, also *sink,* with a note indicating a num-
ber of variant meanings, several related to the idea of *decay;* G,
attain. **323** The translators have not managed the alliteration, *d* in
the original. Savage and Emerson **ma** *makes.* The sense is not sig-
nificantly changed. **324** The translators wish to use the *doom* quite
literally. The judgment will occur on the other side of the stream.
327 forlete loss of word in NE is nearly irreparable. *Now have I
found what I* **forlete.** **328 fyne** lost in the sense of *die.* **330 dotȝ**
verb in text omitted in translation. **334 Ne how fer of folde þat
man mey fleme** lit., *Nor how far from the land men may drive me.*
335 perleȝ O, *pearl;* G, no gloss; H, *peerless one.* MS emended from
perleȝ to **perle;** G holds that this is demanded by the context. H, no
note.

29

Thow demeȝ noȝt bot doel dystresse
Þenne sayde þat wyȝt why dotȝ þou so
For dyne of doel of lureȝ lesse
340 Ofte mony mon forgos þe mo
Þe oȝte better þyseluen blesse
& loue ay God & wele & wo
For anger gayneȝ þe not a cresse
Who nedeȝ schal þole be not so þro
345 For þoȝ þou daunce as any do
Braundysch & bray þy braþeȝ breme
When þou no fyrre may to ne fro
Þou moste abyde þat he schal deme

30

Deme dryȝtyn euer hym adyte
350 Of þe way a fote ne wyl he wryþe
Þy mendeȝ mounteȝ not a myte
Þaȝ þou for sorȝe be neuer blyþe
Stynst of þy strot & fyne to flyte
& sech hys blyþe ful swefte & swyþe
355 Þy prayer may hys pyte byte
Þat mercy schal hyr crafteȝ kyþe
Hys comforte may þy langour lyþe
& þy lureȝ of lyȝtly leme
For marre oþer madde morne & myþe
360 Al lys in hym to dyȝt & deme

---

337 Alliteration on *d* is lost. 339 dyne of doel See l. 51. lureȝ lesse
H, *minor loss*—to refer to material things; G, *sorrows*. The trans-
lators assume that the line referred to material things, not to grief
or bereavement. 343 Translation is literal. 344 þro O, *impatient;*
G, *stubborn;* H, *fierce.* be not so þro has been reversed from nega-
tive to positive. 346 braundysch O and G, *struggle;* H, *threaten.*
brabeȝ O, *violence;* G, *agonies, violent grief;* H, *furies.* breme O,
raging; G, *fierce, wild;* H, *wild.* 351 mendeȝ O, *reparation;* G,
recompense; H, *opinions, thoughts.* The translators do not think the

29

"Thou deemest naught but grief's distress?"
Then said my pearl, "Why dost thou so?
By wailing over worthlessness
Much more do many men forego.   340
Thou wouldst do better thyself to bless,
To love God always in weal and woe,
For anger gainest thee not a cress;
Thou needst must suffer. Be still, for though
Thou ragest and dancest like any doe,   345
Struggle and bray, in fury scream—
When thou canst no further, to or fro,
Thou must abide what He shall deem.

30

"Deem thy Lord, Him long indict:
No foot will He falter nor turn from His way;   350
Thy judgments matter not a mite
Though thou for grief be never gay.
Cease thy strife; no longer fight,
And fervently His favor pray.
Thy prayer His pity may invite   355
That mercy will its power display.
His comfort thy sorrows can allay
And lighten thy losses so joy may gleam,
For rage and rave, or hide away
Thy hurt, all lies in Him to deem."   360

interpretations of O or G make sense in the context of this line.
355 byte O, *lay hold upon;* G, *bite, prick, move;* H, *secure.* **358 & þy
lureȝ of lyȝtly leme** O, *and beat off thy frowns easily.* But in 1. 339
O gives *losses,* mentioning the possibility of *frowns.* G, *sorrows,* but
gives **fleme** for **leme** as reading; H, *losses,* **leme** *gleam brightly;*
Emerson, *And comfort may easily shine out of thy losses.* **359
myþe** O, *escape;* G and Savage, *conceal* (one's feelings). The trans-
lators think they have correctly interpreted both G and H.

VII   31

Thenne demed I to þat damyselle
Ne worþe no wrathþe vnto my Lorde
If raþely [I] raue spornande in spelle
My herte watȝ al wyth mysse remorde
365 As wallande water gotȝ out of welle
I do me ay in hys myserecorde
Rebuke me neuer wyth wordeȝ felle
Þaȝ I forloyne my dere endorde
Bot lyþeȝ me kyndely your coumforde
370 Pytosly þenkande vpon þysse
Of care & me ȝe made acorde
Þat er watȝ grounde of alle my blysse

32

My blysse my bale ȝe han ben boþe
Bot much þe bygger ȝet watȝ my mon
375 Fro þou watȝ wroken fro vch a woþe
I wyste neuer quere my perle watȝ gon
Now I hit se now leþeȝ my loþe
& quen we departed we wern at on
God forbede we be now wroþe
380 We meten so selden by stok oþer ston
Þaȝ cortaysly ȝe carp con
I am bot mol & mare reȝ mysse
Bot Crystes mersy & Mary & Jon
Þise arn þe grounde of alle my blysse

362 G translates *Let my Lord be not offended.*   **363 raþely** omitted
in translation. O translates it as *hastily, quickly;* G, *rashly;* H, *reck-*
lessly.   **364 remorde** O, *stricken with remorse;* G, H, *afflicted.* G, *my*
heart was all afflicted with a sense of loss like gushing water that runs
from a fountain. H translated *afflicted* in gloss, but l. 364 *my heart*
was all with loss disturbed.   **365 As wallande water gotȝ out of welle**
lit., *welling water goes out of well,* but the repetition of *well* in NE
sounds unpleasantly repetitive.   **366 I do me ay in hys myserecorde,**
O, H, *place myself in His compassion;* G translated **do** as *put, place.*

VII   31

Then I addressed that demoiselle:
"Against my Lord let no anger be,
If scornful in speech I did rebel,
My heart's remorse most wretchedly
Rose like water from a well.   365
May His mercy comfort me.
Rebuke me not in phrases fell.
My dear, I spoke mistakenly,
But with kind comfort, soothingly,
And, with compassion, think on this: 370
Myself and care to harmony
You brought, once ground of all my bliss.

32

"Thou hast been both my bliss and bale,
But much the bigger was my woe.
When thou wast removed, no search would avail—   375
I knew not where my pearl did go.
Now, looking on thee, no loss can prevail.
One we were when we parted, so
God forbid that now we rail.
So seldom we meet, going to and fro.   380
Though courteously ye discourse so:
I am but dust and manners miss.
May Christ and Mary and John bestow
Their mercy, the ground of all my bliss.

374 mon O, lit., *complaint;* G, *grief;* H, *woe, dole.* **375 fro vch a woþe** O, *from any danger;* G, *peril;* H, *hunt, search;* Savage, *pathway.* Rhyme problem solved by use of *avail.* **379 wroþe** O, *at odds;* G, *angry, at variance;* H, *wroth.* **380 by stok oþer ston** a filler, for *anywhere.* **382** O gives the text as **marereȝ** translated as *butcher, spoiler.* **mysse** *failure, sin: I am worth no more than a botcher's blunder, good for nothing;* H gives **mare reȝ mysse** (**mare** *onrush, eloquence*) and explains the loss of speech in the presence of God; G, **manereȝ** *manners, courtesy,* no note.

33

385 In blysse I se þe blyþely blent
    & I a man al mornyf mate
    Ȝe take þeron ful lyttel tente
    Þaȝ I hente ofte harmeȝ hate
    Bot now I am here in your presente
390 I wolde bysech wythouten debate
    Ȝe wolde me say in sobre asente
    What lyf ȝe lede erly & late
    For I am ful fayn þat your astate
    Is worþen to worschyp & wele iwysse
395 Of alle my joy þe hyȝe gate
    Hit is in grounde of alle my blysse.

34

    Now blysse burne mot þe bytyde
    Þen sayde þat lufsoum of lyth & lere
    & welcum here to walk & byde
400 For now þy speche is to me dere
    Maysterful mod & hyȝe pryde
    I hete þe arn heterly hated here
    My Lorde ne loueȝ not for to chyde
    For meke arn all þat woneȝ hym nere
405 & when in hys place þou schal apere
    Be dep deuote in hol mekenesse
    My Lorde þe lamb loueȝ ay such chere
    Þat is þe grounde of alle my blysse

---

386 mornyf mate O, *mournful, dejected;* G, *sorrowful, dejected;* H, *mournful, balked, And I a man all mournful balked.* **393** We have lost all alliteration on *f* of **ful fayn** to prevent too much archaizing (see *wis,* l. 394). **394 worschyp** O, *distinction;* G, H, *honor.* **395** There is no way to translate **gate** as *way* or *road.* We have substituted the somewhat inexact *state,* since the dreamer has not yet attained heaven or grace, but is only on the way to it. He recognizes

33

"In bliss I see thee blithely blent   385
And I a man in mourning wait.
You little heed my heart's lament;
My burning griefs oft subjugate
Me. Now before you I am sent:
I would beseech without debate   390
That you would soberly present
What life you lead, early and late,
For I rejoice that your estate
Is changed to worship and weal, I wis;
Of all, my joy, high Heaven's state   395
Is the sure ground of all my bliss."

34

"Now, noble sir, bliss thee betide,"
Then said that lovely of limb, "for here
Art thou welcome to walk and bide,
For now to me thy speech is dear.   400
Masterful mood and haughty pride
I warn thee are hotly hated. Fear
My Lord who lovest not to chide,
For meek are all men dwelling near.
And when in His palace thou shalt appear,   405
Be deeply devout in submissiveness;
My Lord the Lamb loves aye such cheer
That is the ground of all my bliss.

this *state* as the *ground of bliss*. **398 lyth & lere** O, G, *limb and face;* **lyth** H, *form.* **401 mod** O, *mind, temper;* G, H, *mood. Fear* is introduced for rhyme, but is not contrary to the sense of the whole. **402 heterly** O, *bitterly;* G, H, *strongly.* If glossed as *promise,* as by Emerson and Savage, the translation is not clear. **406 hol mekenesse** O, *whole, entire meekness;* G, *complete meekness;* H, *entire, all meekness.*

35

A blysful lyf þou says I lede
410 Þou woldeȝ knaw þerof þe stage
Þow wost wel when þy perle con schede
I watȝ ful ȝong & tender of age
Bot my Lorde þe lombe þurȝ hys godhede
He toke my self to hys maryage
415 Corounde me quene in blysse to brede
In lenghe of dayeȝ þat euer schal wage
& sesed in alle hys herytage
Hys lef is I am holy hysse
Hys prese hys prys & hys parage
420 Is rote & grounde of alle my blysse

VIII   36 *

Blysful quod I may þys be trwe
Dyspleseȝ not if I speke errour
Art þou þe quene of heueneȝ blwe
Þat al þys worlde schal do honour
425 We leuen on Marye þat grace of grewe
Þat ber a barne of vyrgynflor
Þe croune fro hyr quo moȝt remwe
Bot ho hir passed in sum fauour
Now for synglerty o hyr dousour
430 We calle hyr fenyx of arraby
Þat freles fleȝe of hyr fasor
Lyk to þe quen of cortaysye

---

409 *dell* introduced as a rhyme word. The sense is carried over to
l. 410. **410 stage** O, *rank, degree of advancement;* G, H, *state, ad-
vancement.* **413 godhede,** lit., *Godhead,* causing problem in rhym-
ing. **415 to brede** O, *to dwell;* G, *to grow, to flourish;* H, no gloss.
416 þat euer schal wage O, *that ever shall endure;* G, *continue se-
curely, bring reward;* H, *keep troth or faith.* **418 Hys lef is** O, G,
H, *is his beloved.* **419 Hys prese hys prys & hys parage** O, *great
value, excellence, noble lineage;* G, *great worth, excellence, high
lineage;* H, *virtue, merit, value, majesty, nobility. Seest thou* dictated
by rhyme; it omits the idea of the nobility of Christ.

* For stanza 36 the translators tried minor accent in the *b* rhymes,
as done in the original. In this way it was possible to stay very close
to the text.

35

"What blissful life down in this dell
Wouldst thou say I lead and ask me how.   410
Fully thou knewest, when thy pearl fell,
I was young and tender of years, but now
My Lord the Lamb through His holy spell
Took me to Himself by marriage vow,
Crowned me His queen in bliss to dwell   415
To the end of days, did me endow
With His heritage. He did allow
Me the beloved. I am wholly His.
His value, His virtue (seest thou),
Are root and ground of all my bliss."   420

VIII   36 *

"Blessed," quoth I, "may this be true?
Be not displeased if I speak in error.
Art thou the Queen of heaven's blue
Whom all this world must hold in honor?
We trust in Mary, from whom grace grew   425
That bore a babe in virgin flower.
Who would uncrown the Virgin? Who
But one who surpassed her in some favor?
Now for the rareness of her douceur
We call her the Phoenix of Araby,   430
That flawless flew from her Creator
Like to the Queen of Courtesy."

---

425 þat grace of grewe O is not sure whether Christ or Mary is
intended as the source of grace; G, no note; H, Mary *from whom
sprang Grace,* that is, Jesus Christ. The translators think that Mary
was the Virgin Mother of Christ by Grace, but, in another sense,
Christ (Grace) took human form from the Virgin.   **427 Þe croune
fro hyr quo moȝt remwe** *Who might remove the crown from her.*
429 synglerty O, G, *uniqueness, preeminence;* H, *singularity, unique
quality.* **douceur** O, G, H, *sweetness, loveliness.*   **431 Þat freles fleȝe
of hyr fasor** O, *That blameless flew from her appearance,* no note;
G, *That flawless flew from her Creator.* G's note indicates that this
translation is based on the idea that Mary was immaculate from the
moment of her conception; H, *That flawless flew from her Maker/
Creator.*

37

Cortayse quen þenne s[a]yde þat gaye
Knelande to grounde folde vp hyr face
435 Makeleȝ moder & myryest may
Blessed bygyner of vch a grace
Þenne ros ho vp & con restay
& speke me towarde in þat space
Sir fele here porchaseȝ & fongeȝ pray
440 Bot supplantoreȝ none wythinne þys place
Þat emperise al heuen[e]ȝ hatȝ
& vrþe & helle in her bayly
Of erytage ȝet non wyl ho chace
For ho is quen of cortaysye

38 *

445 The court of þe kyndom of God alyue
Hatȝ a property in hyt self beyng
Alle þat may þerinne aryue
Of alle þe reme is quen oþer kyng
& neuer oþer ȝet schal depryue
450 Bot vchon fayn of opereȝ hafyng
& wolde her corouneȝ wern worþe þo fyue
If possyble were her mendyng
Bot my lady of quom Jesu con spryng
Ho haldeȝ þe empyre ouer vus ful hyȝe
455 & þat dyspleseȝ non of oure gyng
For ho is quene of cortaysye

---

433 gaye O, *radiant, joyous one;* G, *fair damsel;* H, *bright one.*
434 Savage, *The turning of her face upwards in devotion;* H, *her face concealed.* **437-438 & con restay** O, G, *pause;* H, *restrain, and was able to restrain and contradict me in that interval.* The translators believe that theirs is a more accurate translation. **439 porchaseȝ & fongeȝ pray** O, *acquire with effort & get prey?* G, *many contest here and win the prize,* **pray** *prize won in contest;* H, *many seek and attain reward.* **443 Of erytage ȝet non wyl ho chace** G,

37

"Courteous Queen," that gay one said,
Kneeling low, concealing her face,
"Matchless Mother and merriest Maid,   435
Blessed Beginner of every grace."
Then she arose; my words were stayed.
She spoke to me across that space,
"Sir, many who seek here, here are paid.
But no usurpers may know this place.   440
That Empress doth all Heaven embrace
And Earth and Hell in her empery.
No heritage will she ever efface,
For she is Queen of Courtesy.

38 *

"The court of the Kingdom of God alive   445
Holds to this law of its very being:
Each one that may therein arrive
Of all the realm is queen or king.
No one shall ever another deprive,
But each one joys in the other's having.   450
They would that another's crown were five,
If it were possible, their amending.
But my Lady from whom Jesus did spring
Holds empire over us so high,
Which displeases none of our gathering,   455
For she is the Queen of Courtesy.

Of heritage yet none will she oust; H, *drive out.*

* As in the original, the major and minor accent rhyme has been
used in the *b* group.

447 The text has **alle;** however, since it is the subject of *is queen or
king* in the next line, it was difficult to translate. **450** Ll. 450 and
451 mean: if it were possible to improve heavenly crowns, each one
would be five times as good.

39

Of courtaysye as saytʒ saynt poule
Al arn we membreʒ of Jesu Kryst
As heued & arme & legg & naule
460 Temen to hys body ful trwe & t[r]yste
Ryʒt so is vch a Krysten sawle
A longande lym to þe mayster of myste
Þenne loke what hate oþer any gawle
Is tached oþer tyʒed þy lymmeʒ bytwyste
465 Þy heued hatʒ nauþer greme ne gryste
On arme oþer fynger þaʒ þou ber byʒe
So fare we alle wyth luf & lyste
To kyng & quene by cortaysye

40

Cortayse quod I I leue
470 & charyte gret be yow among
Bot my speche þat yow ne greue

●   ●   ●   ●   ●   ●

Þyself in heuen ouer hyʒ þou heue
To make þe quen þat watʒ so ʒonge
475 What more honour moʒte he acheue
Þat hade endured in worlde stronge
& lyued in penaunce hys lyueʒ longe
Wyth bodyly bale hym blysse to byye
What more worschyp moʒt he fonge
480 Þen corounde be kyng by cortayse

---

457 "Courtesy" is not the word used in I Corinthians 12:12-31. The author here uses it in its highest mediaeval meaning: the sensitive appreciation of each person for others. **459 naule** O, *nail;* G and H, *navel.* The figure is a powerful one, but difficult to translate without rendering it ludicrous. **460 t[r]yste** G, *faithfully;* H, *trusted, tried;* O thinks the reading is **tyste** *tight.* **462 myste** O, *might, power;* G, *spiritual mysteries;* H, *might, power, strength;* Wright, *graciousness, courtesy,* as in l. 468. **464 lymmeʒ** lit., *limbs* (carry-

39

"Through courtesy, as saith St. Paul,
All members of Jesus Christ are we,
As head and arm and leg, and all
Bound to His body steadfastly,   460
Just so is every Christian soul
A limb of the Master of mystery.
Consider then, whether hate or gall
Is fixed or fast in thy company.
Thy head no wrath nor rancor may see,   465
Whether arm or finger adorned be,
So go we all with love and glee
As king and queen by courtesy."

40

"Courtesy," quoth I, "I do believe,
And among you charity may be great.   470
But at my speech you should not grieve

❀   ❀   ❀   ❀   ❀   ❀

Too high in heaven you misconceive
Yourself, so young, to a queen's estate.
What greater honor might one achieve   475
Who endured in the world, and dedicate
His life to penance long, to rate
From bodily bale true sanctity?
Who might his worship elevate
Above a king's in courtesy?   480

ing out the figure of the members of Jesus Christ). **466 byƷe** O,
finger-ring or *bracelet;* G, H, *ring.* The alliteration on *b* has been
lost. **472** This line is missing in the original text. Gollancz, [**Me
þynk þou spekeƷ now ful wronge**]. **476 stronge** lit., *strongly;* O
says *Who has endured* (*trial*) *in a violent world, . . . who has
continued strong in this world;* G, *Who had endured* (that is, *re-
mained*) *steadfast in the world;* H's gloss, *strong.* **478 to byye** O,
G, H, *to buy.* **479 fonge** O, *get, gain;* G, *take, receive;* H, *attain.*

IX   41

That cortayse is to fre of dede
Ȝyf hyt be soth þat þou coneȝ saye
Þou lyfed not two ȝer in oure þede
Þou cowþes neuer God nauþer plese ne pray
485 Ne neuer nawþer Pater ne Crede
& quen mad on þe fyrst day
I may not traw so God me spede
Þat God wolde wryþe so wrange away
Of countes damysel par ma fay
490 Wer fayr in heuen to halde asstate
Oþen elleȝ a lady of lasse aray
Bot a quene hit is to dere a date

42

Þer is no date of hys godnesse
Þen sayde to me þat worþy wyȝte
495 For all is trawþe þat he con dresse
& he may do noþynk bot ryȝt
As Mathew meleȝ in your messe
In sothfol gospel of God Almyȝt
In sample he can ful grayþely gesse
500 & lykneȝ hit to heuen lyȝte
My regne he saytȝ is lyk on hyȝt
To a lorde þat hade a uyne I wate
Of tyme of ȝere þe terme watȝ tyȝt
To labor vyne watȝ dere þe date

---

487 This looks like a forced rhyme; it is a literal translation. **488 wryþe** O, *turn, as in active work or exercise;* G, *turn so unjustly from the true path;* H, *deviate.* The alliteration on *r* has been lost. **495 dresse** O, *order;* G, *ordain;* H, *establish.* **499 grayþely** O, *ex-*

IX   41

"That courtesy is too free indeed,
If it be sooth, what thou dost say.
Not two years' life with us didst lead,
Never to please God, nor to pray;
Thou knewest neither Pater nor Creed—   485
And to be a Queen the very first day!
I cannot believe, so God me speed,
That God would turn to so wrong a way.
A countess, damsel, by my fay,
Were fair in Heaven to hold estate,   490
Or else a lady of less array,
But a queen—it is too soon a date."

42

"There is no date to His goodliness,"
Then said to me that maiden white,
"For all is truth that His words stress,   495
And He may do no thing but right.
In your Mass, as Matthew doth profess,
In the truthful Gospel, the God of Might,
In His parable doth well express
And likens the tale to celestial light: 500
'My realm,' He saith, 'in Heaven's height
Is like to a lord whose vineyards wait
In the term of the year when the time was quite
Near to the harvest, the proper date.'

---

actly; G, aptly; H, readily. **502 a lorde þat hade a uyne I wate**
a lord that had a vineyard I know; wate know, not *wait.* **503 tyȝt**
O, *come;* G, H, *arrived.* **504 dere** lit., *time was precious;* G, *good;*
O, *urgent;* H, *precious.* The alliteration on *d* has been dropped.

43

505 Þat date of ȝere wel knawe þys hyne
Þe lorde ful erly vp he ros
To hyre werkmen to hys vyne
& fyndeȝ þer summe to hys porpos
Into acorde þay con declyne
510 For a pene on a day & forth þay gotȝ
Wryþen & worchen & don gret pyne
Keruen & caggen & man hit clos
Aboute vnder þe lorde to marked totȝ
& ydel men stande he fyndeȝ þerate
515 Why stande ȝe ydel he sayde to þos
Ne knawe ȝe of þis day no date

44

Er date of daye hider arn we wonne
So watȝ al samen her answar soȝt
We haf standen her syn ros þe sunne
520 & no mon byddeȝ vus do ryȝt noȝt
Gos into my vyne dotȝ þat ȝe conneȝ
So sayde þe lorde & made hit toȝt
What resonable hyre be naȝt be runne
I yow pray in dede & þoȝte
525 Þay wente into þe vyne & wroȝte
& al day þe lorde þus ȝede his gate
& nw men to hys vyne he broȝte
Welneȝ wyl day watȝ passed date

---

505 hyne H, *householders;* G, O, Savage, *laborers.* **511 don gret pyne** O, *do great exertion;* G, *toil;* H, *pain.* **512 caggen** O, *bind;* G, *tie up;* H, *bind.* **man hit clos** H, lit., *gather the harvest.* **514 gate** has been supplied for the rhyme. **516** Translation loses alliteration on *d* in text. **517** Text alliterates on *d,* **date of daye.** **518 soȝt**

43

"Laborers know of that season the signs: 505
That very early the lord arose
To hire the harvesters for his vines,
And some, who suited his purpose, chose.
Into agreement each one consigns
Himself for a penny a day, and those   510
Go forth to travail and toil, ere shines
The sun, to cut and reap the rows.
The master at three to the market goes,
Where he finds men idle at the gate:
'Why stand ye idle? No man knows,'   515
He questions them, 'the hour or date?'

44

" 'We came here ere the break of day.'
So was their answer in chorus sighed,
'Here we have stood since the sun's first ray,
And no man bids us to his side.'   520
'Go to my vineyard; do what you may,'
So said the lord, 'this bond abide:
I vow in thought and deed to pay
The wage you win by eventide.'
Into his vineyard then they hied.   525
All day the lord went his own gait
And new men for his vines supplied
Till well nigh past was that day's date.

O, H, *sighed;* G, *sought.* **520 do ryȝt noȝt** *do nothing at all.* **521 conneȝ** lit., *can.* **522-524** These lines are partially transposed, from the original, and put immediately into direct discourse. In the text, the lord's speech begins at l. 524. **523** This argument is a difficult one. **524 pray** clearly given in MS and H; O, G, **pay.**

45

At þe day of date of euensonge
530 On oure byfore þe soone go doun
He seʒ þer ydel men ful stronge
& sade to hem wyth sobre soun
Wy stonde ʒe ydel þise dayeʒ longe
Þay sayden her hyre watʒ nawhere boun
535 Gotʒ to my vyne ʒeman ʒonge
& wyrkeʒ & dotʒ þat at ʒe moun
Sone þe worlde bycom wel broun
Þe sunne watʒ doun & & hit wex late
To take her hyre he mad sumoun
540 Þe day watʒ al apassed date

X   46

The date of þe daye þe lorde con knaw
Called to þe reue lede pay þe meyny
Gyf hem þe hyre þat I hem owe
& fyrre þat non me may reprene
545 Set hem alle vpon a rawe
& gyf vchon inlyche a peny
Bygyn at þe laste þat standeʒ lowe
Tyl to þe fyrste þat þou atteny
& þenne þe fyrst bygonne to pleny
550 & sayden þat þay had trauayled sore
Þese bot on oure hem con streny
Vus þynk vus oʒe to take more

---

529 Text alliterates on *d,* but the use of **date** for time is no longer appropriate.   **534 Þay sayden her hyre watʒ nawhere boun** O, *Their hire was nowhere ready; their service was nowhere engaged;* G and H have no notes about this line.   **536 dotʒ þat at ʒe moun** O, *do what you may;* G, H, *do what you can.*   **541** The translation lacks alliteration; the text alliterates on *d.*   **543** The text alliterates on *h.* **546 inlyche** G, *alike;* H, Hamilton (*The Journal of English and Germanic Philology,* LVII, 2, 188–189) *fully.* Matthew 20:10 "And

45

"At the time of day for evensong,
An hour before the sun had downed,   530
He saw there idle men and strong
And spoke to them with sober sound:
'Why stand ye idle the whole day long?'
'No contract yet our time has bound.'
'Young yeomen, to my vineyard throng   535
And do the work that can be found.'
Darkness soon the world embrowned;
The sun was set and it grew late.
To pay their wage he called them 'round,
And the day was all a passèd date.   540

X   46

"When the lord the time of day did know,
He called to the reeve, 'Pay the company.
Give them their wages, whatever I owe,
And further, that none find fault with me,
Stand them all up in a row   545
And give each one alike a penny.
Begin with the last who stands down low,
Until you come to the first of the many.'
But the first protested. Unfailingly,
They said, they had worked and travailed sore.   550
'While these have worked but one hour only.
It seems to us we should get more.'

they likewise received every man a penny." The translators think
that **inlyche** in l. 603 also means *alike*, that is, the same amount, as
the Bible suggests, though the number of hours worked was different.
547 þat standeȝ lowe O, lit., *who stands low (in rank of order)*.
548-549 *the first*, repeated in ll. 548 and 549. H notes that the ME
is artificial and was used to supply the rhyme. **pleny** *began to com-
plain.*

47

More haf we serued vus þynk so
Þat suffred han þe dayeȝ hete
555 Þenn þyse þat wroȝt not houreȝ two
& þou dotȝ hem vus to counterfete
Þenne sayde þe lorde to on of þo
Frende no wanig I wyl þe ȝete
Take þat is þyn owne & go
560 & I hyred þe for a peny agrete
Quy bygynneȝ þou now to þrete
Watȝ not a pene þy couenaunt þore
Fyrre þen couenaunde is noȝt to plete
Wy shalte þou þenne ask more

48

565 More weþer louyly is me my gyfte
To do wyth myn quat so me lykeȝ
Oþer elleȝ þyn yȝe to lyþer is lyfte
For I am goude & non byswykeȝ
Þus schal I quod Kryste hit skyfte
570 Þe laste schal be þe fyrst þat strykeȝ
& þe fyrst þe laste be he neuer so swyft
For mony ben calle þaȝ fewe be mykeȝ
Þus pore men her part ay pykeȝ
Þaȝ þay com late & lyttel wore
575 & þaȝ her sweng wyth lyttel atslykeȝ
Þe merci of God is much þe more

---

555 **Þenn þyse þat wroȝt not houreȝ two** lit., *Than these who have worked not two hours.* 557 **on of þo** lit., *one of those.* Altered for rhyme. 558 **wanig** O, *loss;* G, *curtailment;* H, *lacking.* H is probably correct. 560 **agrete** O, *for the job;* G, *all together, as a body;* H, *agreed.* H is probably correct, but the rhyme is a problem. Savage, *done by the piece.* In the context, this does not seem reasonable. 561 **þrete** O, *complain;* G, *wrangle;* H, *rebuke.* 567 **lyþer . . . lyfte.**

47

" 'More have we served, it seems to us so,
Enduring here the long day's heat,
Than those who began not two hours ago,　　　　555
And thou dost equate us as just and meet.'
Then said the lord to one, 'Although,
My friend, thou chidest, I did not cheat;
Take what is thine own and go.
I hired thee for a penny complete.　　　　560
Why, with grumblings, dost thou greet
Me? A penny was thy contract for.
Beyond our bargain naught entreat.
Why shalt thou then ask for more?'

48

" 'Is it not lawful with my own gift　　　　565
To do whatever I wish to do?
Or else thine eyes to evil lift
Because I am good, guileless, and true?'
'Thus,' quoth Christ, 'I shall portion and shift
The last so he be the first of you,　　　　570
And the first the last, be he never so swift,
For many are called, though the chosen are few.'
Thus poor men always attain their due,
Though the least come late, inferior,
And though their stroke slides down askew,　　　　575
The mercy of God is much the more.

Text has *l* alliteration. The translators use assonance. **570 þat strykeȝ** lit., *that goes;* G, *who comes (for reward).* The line seems to be padded, probably for rhyme. The translators have substituted *first of you.* **571** The alliteration on *s* has been lost in the translation. **573 pykeȝ** O, *plunder, carry off;* G, H, *pick, gather, get.* The sense seems to call for the interpretation of G and H.

49

More haf I of ioye & blysse hereinne
Of ladyschyp gret & lyueȝ blom
Þen alle þe wyȝeȝ in þe worlde myȝt wynne
580 By þe way of ryȝt to aske dome
Wheþer welnygh now I con bygynne
In euentyde into þe vyne I come
Fyrst of my hyre my Lorde con mynne
I watȝ payed anon of al & sum
585 Ȝet oþer þer werne þat toke more tom
Þat swange & swat for long ȝore
Þat ȝet of hyre noþynk þay nom
Paraunter noȝt schal toȝere more

50

Then more I meled & sayde apert
590 Me þynk þy tale vnresounable
Goddeȝ ryȝt is redy & euermore rert
Oþer holy wryt is bot a fable
In sauter is sayd a verce ouerte
Þat spekeȝ a poynt determynable
595 Þou quyteȝ vchon as hys desserte
Þou hyȝe kyng ay pretermynable
Now he þat stod þe long day stable
& þou to payment com hym byfore
Þenne þe lasse in werke to take more able
600 & euer þe lenger þe lasse þe more

---

578 lyueȝ, verb intransitive. **blom** O, *prime*; G, *bloom, perfection. perfection lives? prime lives?* H translates *bloom of life* and notes that **lyueȝ** is genitive of **lyf. 585 tom** O, *had longer to wait*; G, H, *spent more time.* **587** Alliteration on *n* in text. **nom** lit., *received.* This word is lost in NE. **591 rert** O, *roused, awake*; G, *raised, supreme*; H, *established.* **593** Alliteration on *s* in the first two

49

"More joy and bliss have I herein,
With life and ladyship allied,
Than all men in the world might win,
When judged by the way of right as guide.   580
Although just now I did begin—
To the vineyard I came at eventide—
My Lord remembered as I came in,
At once full pay He did provide.
Yet others longer their labor supplied,   585
That toiled and sweated so long of yore,
But by no wages were satisfied—
May not be paid for a long time more."

50

Then I spoke more, frankly essayed,
"Thy accounting seems unreasonable;   590
God's right is ready, forever made,
Or Holy Writ is but a fable.
In the Psalter is the verse displayed
That speaks a point determinable:
By his desert each one is paid,   595
Thou High King aye Preterminable.
Now he that stood the long day stable,
And for the payment thou camest before
Him, to work the less, to earn more able,
And ever the longer, the less the more."   600

stresses and on *v* in the last two. **596 pretermynable** O, G, *fore-ordaining*; H, *Infinite, Eternal* from L. **prae terminabilis.** The text has perfect rhymes in ll. 590, 594, and 596. **597 stable** O, *steady;* G, *steadfast;* H, *firm.* **600** G, *continually the less* (*work done*) . . . *the more* (*able to earn*).

XI   51 *

Of more & lasse in Godeʒ ryche
Þat gentyl sayde lys no joparde
For þer is vch mon payed inlyche
Wheþer lyttel oþer much be hys rewarde
605 For þe gentyl cheuentayn is no chyche
Queþersoeuer he dele nesch oþer harde
He laueʒ hys gyfteʒ as water of dyche
Oþer goteʒ of golf þat neuer charde
Hys fraunchyse is large þat euer dard
610 To hym þat matʒ in synne rescoghe
No blysse betʒ fro hem reparde
For þe grace of God is gret inoghe

52

Bot now þou moteʒ me for to mate
Þat I my peny haf wrang tan here
615 Þou sayʒ þat I þat come to late
Am not worþy so gret lere
Where wysteʒ þou euer any bourne abate
Euer so holy in hys prayere
Þat he ne forfeted by sum kyn gate
620 Þe mede sumtyme of heueneʒ clere
& ay þe ofter þe alder þay were
Þay laften ryʒt & wroʒten woghe
Mercy and grace moste hem þen stere
For þe grace of God is gret innoʒe

---

* The first four lines of this stanza are transposed as follows: 2 → 1, 1 → 2, 3 → 4, 4 → 3.

603 See note on l. 546.   **604 rewarde** O, *reward;* G, Savage, *estimation, due recognition of merit;* H, *reward.*   **605 For þe gentyl cheuentayn is no chyche** *For the gentle Lord is no niggard.*   **606 nesch** O, *tenderly;* G, *soft, pleasant.*   **608 goteʒ** O, G, *streams.* **golf** O, *body of deep water;* G, *space underground (as a source of a stream).* **charde** O, *cease;* G, *turned back, ceased to flow.*   **609-610 dard** G, *shrank in fear before? lay hidden, was inscrutable?* There are long notes by the commentators. H translates *Ample is his heritage who always reverence paid to Him who makes rescue in the case of sin.* The explanation of **dard** as both *to be hidden* and *to be in awe of* seems reasonable, but **fraunchyse** is surely *generosity* rather than

XI   51

"Of more and less in the Lord's domain
There is no doubt," said that gentle maid,
"Whether little or much be his due gain,
For there each man is equally paid.
No miser is the Master—in vain   605
His dealings, mild or harsh, are weighed.
Like water undammed His dear gifts rain,
Or streams that from their source cascade.
His gifts are generously displayed
To those who fear Him. He will slough   610
Off their sins in joy unstayed,
For the grace of God is great enough.

52

"My argument to abnegate,
Thou sayest my penny inequitably
I earned, and that I came too late   615
And am not worth so great a fee.
Whenever men their zeal abate,
However pious their prayers may be,
They forfeit some of their estate,
The reward of Heaven's brilliancy.   620
Ever more often the older they be
They abandon the right way, narrow and rough;
Mercy and grace must then decree
That the grace of God is great enough.

---

heritage. Savage, *gush out, pour forth*. **rescoghe** O, *delivers;* G, *res-
cue;* H, *rescue*.   **611** Alliteration on *b* is lost.   **613** O, *But now thou
mayst checkmate me;* G, *But now thou mayst shame me;* H, *But now
thou dost argue me to defeat*.   **616** [h]**ere** O, *wages;* **fere** G, *fortune,
rank, dignity*. G says form of **here** not known. **lere** (MS) not in con-
text. May also mean *company*. H uses **lere** *recompense*, from **lure**
lure, compensation, recompense.   **617 abate** O, *endure;* G, verb,
remained, endured; H, *to lose;* Emerson, Savage *to be humbled*. **H**
has a long note indicating that even the pious lose, at times, the de-
votion to God, even though their prayers continue.

53

625 But innoghe of grace hatȝ innocent
As sone as þay arn borne by lyne
In þe water of babtem þay dyssente
Þen arne þay boroȝt into þe vyne
Anon þe day wyth derk endente
630 Þe myȝt of deth dotȝ to enclyne
Þat wroȝt neuer wrang er þenne þay wente
Þe gentyle Lorde þenne payeȝ hys hyne
Þay dyden hys heste þay wern þereine
Why schulde he not her labour alow
635 Ȝys & þay hem at the fyrst fyne
For þe grace of God is gret innoghe

54

Inoȝe is knawen þat mankyn grete
Fyrste watȝ wroȝt to blysse parfyt
Oure forme fader hit con forfete
640 Þurȝ an apple þat he vpon con byte
Al wer we dampned for þat mete
To dyȝe in doel out of delyt
& syþen wende to helle hete
Þerinne to won wythoute respyt
645 Bot þeron com a bote as tyt
Ryche blod ran on rode so roghe
& wynne water þen at þat plyt
Þe grace of God wex gret innoghe

---

625 The translators have altered G's punctuation. A new-born child is not innocent until baptized, see Hamilton, *The Journal of English and Germanic Philology*, LVII, 2; 189. **626** O and G, *in regular order;* H, *in order of birth.* **627** There is no alliteration in the text. **628** There is no alliteration in the text. **629-630 endente** O, G, *inlaid;* O translates *Anon the day, indented with darkness, doth yield to the power of death.* **630** G thinks the word is **nlyȝt** and therefore translates *night of death.* H, O, Savage, **myȝt.** **632** Lit., *gentle Lord.*

53

"But enough of grace have the innocent;   625
As soon as babes are born, by line
Of birth to baptism, their descent
They take, and then they tend the vine.
Forthwith the day with dark accent
Doth to the night of death incline.   630
Who wrought no wrong before they went,
He pays, His servants, Lord divine,
And His behest none did decline.
Why should He their toil rebuff
To pay at the first furrow's fine?   635
For the grace of God is great enough.

54

"Mankind, as well enough we know,
First was wrought to bliss aright.
Our former father then fell so low
Through an apple that he did bite.   640
We all were damned by that fruit of woe,
To die in dolor away from delight,
Then to the heat of hell to go,
Therein to dwell without respite.
But thence there came a cure forthright: 645
Rich blood ran on the rood so rough
And blessèd water: then at that plight
The grace of God grew great enough.

---

635 G, *Pay them at first*, or *in full*; H, *Pay them at the first furrow's end*.   639 **forfete** O, G, H, *forfeit*.   645 Pronunciation change has cost us the accuracy of this rhyme. **þeron** O, no gloss; G, *after that*; H, *for that, thereon*.   647 **at** O, *beside, according to* (?); G, H, **at.** H's note: "At the moment of our Lord's death on the cross grace from God increased for mankind." The alliteration on *w* has been lost in translation.

55

Innoghe þer wax out of þat welle
650 Blod & water of brode wounde
Þe blod vus boȝt fro bale of helle
& delyuered vus of þe deth secounde
Þe water is baptem þe soþe to telle
Þat folȝed þe glayue so grymly grounde
655 Þat wascheȝ away þe gylteȝ felle
Þat Adam wyth inne deth vus drounde
Now is þer noȝt in þe worlde rounde
Bytwene vus & blysse bot þat he wythdroȝ
& þat is restored in sely stounde
660 & þe grace of God is gret innogh

XII   56 *

Grace innogh þe mon may haue
Þat synneȝ þenne new ȝif hym repente
Bot wyth sore & syt he mot hit craue
& byde þe payne þerto is bent
665 Bot resoun of ryȝt þat con not raue
Saueȝ euermore þe innossent
Hit is a dom þat neuer God gaue
Þat euer þe gyltleȝ schulde be schente
Þe gyltyf may contryssyoun hente
670 & be þurȝ mercy to grace þryȝt
Bot he to gyle þat neuer glente
At inoscente is saf & ryȝte

---

654 Meaning? O says "common epithet of weapons in alliterative poems." G and H translate it thus. **658 he,** as H comments, surely refers to Adam, by whose sin mankind lost happiness; this loss was restored by baptism.

* O's note: "The doctrine of this passage may be briefly summarized thus: Salvation is granted both to the innocent and the contrite. The innocent ever possess it as their right; the contrite obtain it only through repentance, the pain of remorse, and the grace and mercy of God. It is better, if one can, to win salvation by innocence, than to

55

"Enough there flowed forth from that well,
Blood and water from wound unbound: 650
The blood that bought us from bale of hell,
From the second death deliverance found.
The water is baptism, truth to tell—
That followed the lance so grimly ground.
It washes away the guilt so fell,   655
In which by Adam in death we drowned.
Now is there naught in the whole world round,
Between us and bliss but that he cast off,
And that is restored in a bliss profound,
And the grace of God is great enough.   660

XII   56 *

"Grace be enough, but sins deprave;
Man errs anew, though he repent.
With sorrow and sighing he must crave
Grace, and serve the penance sent,
But reasoned righteousness naught can waive   665
Saves evermore the innocent.
It is a doom God never gave:
To grieve the guiltless He never meant.
Contrite, the guilty may relent
And through His mercy grace invite,   670
But he whom sin did not torment
With the innocent is safe, by right.

run the risk of failure and the danger of judgment which the other
course involves."

669 Lit., *The guilty may experience contrition.* **670** þryȝt O, G,
through His mercy thrust into grace; H, *impelled.* **671** The allitera-
tion on *g* has been lost in translation. **672** At O, scribal error for
þat; G emends to **As** *being innocent;* H, *with* and *innocent* as a
noun.

57

Ryȝt þus þus I knaw wel in þis cas
Two men to saue is God by skylle

675 Þe ryȝtwys man schal se hys fa[c]e
Þe harmleȝ haþel schal com hym tylle
Þe sauter hyt satȝ þus in a pace
Lorde quo schal klymbe þy hyȝ hylle
Oþer rest wythinne þy holy place

680 Hymself to onsware he is not dylle
Hondelyngeȝ harme þat dyt not ille
Þat is of hert boþe clene & lyȝt
Þer schal hys step stable stylle
Þe innocent is ay saf by ryȝt

58

685 The ryȝtwys man also sertayn
Aproche he schal þat proper pyle
Þat takeȝ not her lyf in vayne
Ne glauereȝ her nieȝbor wyth no gyle
Of þys ryȝtwys saȝ Salamon playn

690 How kyntly on[o]re con aquyle
By wayeȝ ful streȝt he con hym strayn
& sheued hym þe rengne of God a whyle
As quo says lo ȝon louely yle
Þou may hit wynne if þou be wyȝte

695 Bot hardyly wythoute peryle
Þe innocent is ay saue by ryȝte

---

674 god O, G, *good;* H says "**god** must mean *God*, otherwise **hys** (l. 675) and **hym** (l. 676) lack an antecedent." **skylle** O, G, *reasoning;* H, *judgment.* **675** Savage quotes Wright: "in a true statement" (or "meaning"). This translation must be based on a different reading of MS. **676 haþel** O, G, H, *man,* also *worthy fellow.* The alliteration *h* has been lost in translation. **685 also sertayn** H, *undoubtedly.* **686 proper pyle** The alliteration on *p* has been lost in translation. **687 takeȝ** O, *taketh;* G, *use foolishly, spend in folly;* H, *use, consume.* **688 glauereȝ** O, *flatters;* G, H, *deceives.* **689 saȝ** O, *saw;* G, *says;* H, *saw,* plus note. In spite of G's note, the translators think that *saw* is used in the sense of *perceived.* **690 kyntly** O, *lovingly;* H, *fittingly;* G, (**koyntise**) *wisdom.* **aquyle** O, H, *receives;***

57

"Right, thus I knew well, in this case,
Two men to save is God's great skill:
The righteous man shall see His face;   675
The innocent shall He fulfill.
The Psalter says in a certain space:
'Lord, who shall climb to Thy high hill,
Or rest within Thy holy place?
Swiftly to answer is His will: 680
'He whose hands have done no ill,
That is of heart both clean and light,
There shall his step be stable, still:
The innocent is ay safe by right.

58

" 'The righteous man, I ascertain,   685
He shall approach God's domicile;
Who leadeth not his life in vain
And doth his neighbor not beguile.'
Righteousness, saw Solomon plain,
Can honor earn in fitting style."   690
In ways full straight, she did constrain
Him, to see God's realm a while,
As who says, "Lo, yon lovely isle:
If thou be brave, there thou shalt light."
But, with no danger, by no wile,   695
The innocent is ay saved by right.

G, *obtains.* **How kyntly on[o]re con aquyle.** O interpolates **oure**
[kyng hym], justified by the alliteration. G, **How [koyntise on] oure,**
How Wisdom [Christ] obtained honor [for him]. This reading neces-
sitates reading **ho** for **he** in l. 691. H, *How fittingly honor [he] did*
receive. The translators think that an examination of the MS indi-
cates that the line could properly be emended by interpolating one
omitted *o* for **onore.** In the translation assonance has been substi-
tuted for possible alliteration on *k.*   **694 wyȝte** O, *active, brave;* G, H,
valiant.   **695 hardyly** O, *It may be boldly said, assuredly;* G, H,
boldly, firmly. **peryle** O, *risk;* G, H, *peril, exposure to risks.*

59

Anende ryȝtwys men ȝet satȝ a gome
Dauid in sauter if euer ȝe seȝ hit
Lorde þy seruaunt draȝ neuer to dome
700 For non lyuyande to þe is justyfyet
Forþy to corte quen þou schal com
Þer alle oure causeȝ schal be tryed
Alegge þe ryȝt þou may be innome
By þys ilke spech I haue asspyed
705 Bot he on rode þat blody dyed
Delfully þurȝ hondeȝ þryȝt
Gyue þe to passe when þou arte tryed
By innocens & not by ryȝte

60

Ryȝtwysly quo con rede
710 He loke on bok & be awayed
How Jesus hym welke in areþede
& burneȝ her barneȝ vnto hym brayde
For happe & hele þat fro hym ȝede
To touch her chylder þay fayr hym prayed
715 His dessypeleȝ wyth blame let be hym bede
& wyth her resouneȝ ful fele restayed
Jesus þenne hem swetely sayde
Do way let chylder vnto me tyȝt
To suche is heuenryche arayed
720 Þe innocent is ay saf by ryȝt

---

698 seȝ O, G, H, *saw*. The text from the Psalter is "If ever ye saw it." The alliteration on *s* has been lost in the translation. **699** The alliteration on *d* has been lost in the translation. **702 tryed** is repeated in ll. 702 and 707. **703** H, *If thou plead virtue for thyself, thou mayst be denied.* G has a long note on this and agrees substantially with H. See Dorothy Everett and Naomi D. Hurnard, "Legal Phraseology in a Passage in *Pearl*," *Medium Aevum*, XVI, 1947. **704 asspyed,** in text, O, *descried;* G, *observed;* H, *espied, discovered, discerned.* **706 Delfully** O, G, H, *grievously.* **þryȝt** O, G,

59

"Concerning the righteous, one man thought—
In the Psalter, note what David cried:
'Let not thy servants, Lord, be brought
Before Thee—none is justified.'
When to the court thou comest, caught   700
Where all our causes shall be tried,
Thy right asserted shall be naught,
By this same speech I have descried.
But may He on rood that bloody died,   705
(Through His hands the steely bite)
Grant thee to pass when thou art tried,
Through innocence and not through right.

60

"Let any man who can rightly read
Search the Book and there be taught   710
How Jesus walked with an ancient breed
Who cherished children to Him brought;
For hope and health that from Him speed
His touch upon their young ones sought.
'But let Him be!' the twelve decreed,   715
Their crabbèd speech full many caught,
But Jesus sweetly said, 'Do naught
To stay the children from my sight,
For of such Heaven's realm is wrought.'
The innocent ay is safe by right.   720

---

pierced; H, *afflicted.* **710 awayed** O, G, *instructed;* H, *informed.*
711 arebede O, G, *people of yore;* ·H, *a nation of a former time,
ancient land.* **712** Because of the loss of **burneʒ, barneʒ,** *and* **brayde**
the translators could not effect the alliteration on *b.* **716 resouneʒ,**
lit., *reasons,* but **wyth blame** in l. 715 indicates the impatience oɾ
unkindness of the disciples. **718 tyʒt** O, G, H, *draw, come.* The
translators have combined the sense of ll. 718 and 719. **719 arayed**
O, G, H, *prepared.*

XIII   61 *

Jesus con calle to hym hys mylde
& sayde hys ryche no wyȝ myȝt wynne
Bot he com þyder ryȝt as a chylde
Oþer elleȝ neuer more com þerinne
725 Harmleȝ trwe & vndefylde
Wythouten mote oþer mascle of sulpande synne
Quen such þer cnoken on þe bylde
Tyt schal hem men þe ȝate vnpynne
Þer is þe blys þat con not blynne
730 Þat þe jueler soȝte þurȝ perre pres
& solde alle hys goud boþe wolen & lynne
To bye hym a perle watȝ mascelleȝ

62

This makelleȝ perle þat boȝt is dere
Þe joueler gef fore alle hys god
735 Is lyke þe reme of heuenesse clere
So sayde þe fader of folde & flode
For hit is wemleȝ clene & clere
& endeleȝ rounde & blyþe of mode
& commune to alle þat ryȝtwys were
740 Lo euen in myddeȝ my breste hit stode
My Lorde þe lombe þat schede hys blode
He pyȝt hit þere in token of pes
I rede þe forsake þe worlde wode
& porchace þy perle maskelles

---

* G notes that the group of stanzas 61-66 is not linked to the pre-
ceding group. It is the only group not so linked. G and H debate
over whether **mylde** refers to *children* or *disciples*. Here it has been
translated literally and the ambiguity remains.

724 Translation is literal for **neuer more**. **726 mascle** O, G, H,
spot. **sulpande** O, G, H, *polluting*. **727 bylde** O, *building*; G,
dwelling; H, *house, dwelling*. (On the gates of Heaven? or wall?)
728 Tyt O, G, H, *quickly*. **729 blynne** O, G, H, *cease*. The trans-
lators have kept the sense, but lost the alliteration on *b*. **731** Split
rhyme is not used in original where the word is **lynne**. **733**

XIII   61 *

"Jesus called to Him the mild
And said no man might His realm win,
Unless he come there like a child,
He nevermore should dwell therein.
Innocent, true, and undefiled   725
With mote nor mite of staining sin,
When come knocking the unbeguiled
Quickly men shall the gate unpin.
Unending bliss there is within
That the jeweler sought through gems to procure,   730
Sold all his goods, both wool and lin-
en, to buy him a pearl perfect and pure.

62

"This perfect pearl that is bought so dear
That the jeweler sold his livelihood
Is like the realm of Heaven so clear,   735
So said the Father of earth and flood,
For it is spotless, clean, and clear,
An endless round, and blithe of mood,
And common to all the righteous here.
Lo, in the midst of my breast it stood.   740
My Lord the Lamb that shed His blood,
In token of peace, placed it secure.
Forsake the mad world, so I would
Counsel and purchase the pearl that is pure."

ma[s]keleʒ O, no note; G, editorially emended, perhaps poet de-
liberately played on makeleʒ and maskeleʒ. The final stanza uses
both. H, no note on emendation. There is no alliteration in the
original.   734 The alliteration on g has been lost in the translation.
735 Is lyke þe reme of hƀuenesse clere O, G, *like the realm of clear
heaven*. Gollancz emends to spere; G thinks ON skere (*bright, clear*),
but MS can be defended.   737 clere O, *pure, bright, pellucid;* G, H,
clear, used as terminal rhyme in both ll. 735 and 737.   739 Lit.,
that were righteous.   742 pyʒt O, G, *set;* H, *fixed firmly, set in
place.*   743 wode, lost in NE, hence no alliteration.

63

745 O maskeleȝ perle in perleȝ pure
Þat bereȝ quod I þe perle of prys
Quo formed þe þy fayre fygure
Þat wroȝt þy wede he watȝ ful wys
Þy beaute com neuer of nature
750 Pymalyon paynted neuer þy vys
Ne Arystotel nawþer by hys lettrure
Of carpe þe kynde þese properteȝ
Þy colour passeȝ þe flour de lys
Þyn angel hauyng so clene corteȝ
755 Breue me bryȝt quat kyn offys
Bereȝ þe perle so maskelleȝ

64

My makeleȝ lambe þat al may bete
Quod scho my dere destyne
Me ches to hys make alþaȝ vnmete
760 Sumtyme semed þat assemble
When I wente fro yor worlde wete
He calde me to hys bonerte
Cum hyder to me my lemman swete
For mote ne spot is non in þe
765 He gef me myȝt & als bewte
In hys blod he wesch my wede on dese
& coronde clene in vergynte
& pyȝt me in perleȝ maskelleȝ

746 of prys O, *excellence;* G, *exquisite, precious;* H, *of great price.*
747 Minor accent rhymes are used in the original. 750 vys O, G, H, *face.* 751 lettrure O, *writing, books;* G, *learning, science;* H, *literature, writings.* 753 Lit., *Thy color surpasses the fleur-de-lys.* 754 angel hauyng O, G, *angelic demeanor;* H, *angel-manner.* Note to *Destruction of Troy,* (see note to l. 61) 265, "Your angel-mouth's most melifluate." clene corteȝ O, *pure, gracious;* G, *gracious, without flaw or error;* H, *completely courteous.* 755 offys O, G, *office, position;* H, *office, rank.* G has a note on the difficulty of reading this word in the MS. To the translators, however, it seems to be clearly offys. 757 makeleȝ in MS, but the translators think it is a scribal

63

"O spotless pearl in pearls so pure   745
That beareth," quoth I, "the pearl, the prize,
Who formed for thee thy fair figure?
Who wrought thy raiment was full wise.
Thy beauty was never born of nature;
Pygmalion painted not thy guise,   750
Nor Aristotle's literature
Did thy properties apprise.
With the fleur-de-lys thy color vies,
Thine angel-manner, sweet and sure.
Bright one, I bid thee, what rank, advise   755
Me, beareth the pearl so perfect and pure?"

64

"O spotless Lamb who doth defeat
All ills, my dearest Destiny
Chose me His mate, although unmeet
At first had seemed that unity   760
From the world of woe I did retreat.
He called me to His company:
'Come hither to me, my belovèd sweet;
There is no mote nor spot in thee.'
Might and beauty He gave to me.   765
In His blood He rinsed my robes before
He crowned me clean in virginity,
Adorning me in pearls so pure."

error for **maskeleȝ** since this is the fourth stanza to use this key word.
See, however, note to l. 733.   **bete** O, G, *amend, reform, heal;* H,
vanquish, beat. **760 assemble** O, G, H, *union, marriage.* **761 yor**
O, G, no gloss. Literally the line is: *When I went from* [yor] *wet
world.* (**wete** O, *dank, gloomy;* G, *wet, rainy, damp;* H, *wet, woe*
from OE **wite.** H says *wete* seems forced here.) **762 bonerte** O,
goodness; G, *beatitude;* H, *blessedness.* **763 lemman** This word is
lost, in the religious sense, in NE. **764** There is internal rhyme in
ME and the alliteration is on *n.* **766 on dese** O, G, H, *on dais;* O,
place of honor. **768** The translators are responsible for the ap-
proximate rhyme of *before* and *pure.*

65

Why maskelleȝ bryd þat bryȝt con flambe

770 Þat reiateȝ hatȝ so ryche & ryf

Quat kyn þyng may be þat lambe

Þat þe wolde wedde vnto hys vyf

Ouer alle oþer so hyȝ þou clambe

To lede wyth hym so ladyly lyf

775 So mony a comly onvnder cambe

For Kryst han lyued in much stryf

& þou con alle þo dere outdryf

& fro þat maryag al oþer depres

Al only þyself so stout & styf

780 A makeleȝ may & maskelleȝ

XIV   66

Maskelles quod þat myry quene

Vnblemyst I am wythouten blot

& þat may I wyth mensk menteene

Bot makeleȝ quene þenne sade I not

785 Þe lambes vyueȝ in blysse we bene

A hondred & forty þowsande flot

As in þe Apocalyppeȝ hit is sene

Sant John hem syȝ al in a knot

On þe hyl of Syon þat semly clot

790 Þe apostel hem segh in gostly drem

Arayed to þe weddyng in þat hyl coppe

Þe nwe cyte o Jerusalem

769 As O notes, the author is punning on **bryd** *bride,* and *bird,* since he uses the verb *flambe.* **774 ladyly** O, *befitting a lady;* G, *queenly, exalted;* H, *suitable to a lady, noble.* **775 So mony a comly onvnder cambe** *fair beneath comb.* G notes this as a periphrasis similar to the OE *heard under helme* as *warrior.* H notes it as "a conventional phrase, complimentary to ladies." **777** Rhyme consonant has shifted from *f* to *v.* The word in the text is **outdryf. 779 stout** O, *strong;* G, *valiant;* H, *proud.* **styf** O, *firm;* G, *bold;* H, *strong.* The translators have used up all available rhymes. **780** The translation inevitably loses the pun on **makeleȝ** (*matchless*) and **maskelleȝ** (*spotless*). **783** The strict alliteration on *m* has been

65

"Why, spotless bride who flames so bright,
Possessed of royalty rich and rife, 770
What kind of Lamb is He who might
Wed thee and take thee to His wife?
Above all others thou climbedst the height
To lead with Him so noble a life!
So many, comely combed, did fight 775
For Christ and live in constant strife,
And all those dear ones thou didst drive
Out from that marriage and so assure
Thy place alone, so bold and blithe,
A peerless maid, matchless and pure." 780

XIV 66

"Spotless," quoth that merry queen,
"Unblemished I am, without a blot,
And that I may bear with stately mien,
But 'unmatched queen,' that said I not.
All wives of the Lamb in bliss we have been, 785
A hundred and forty thousand lot,
As in the Apocalypse it is seen.
St. John saw them gathered all in a knot,
On the hill of Sion, that seemly spot.
The Apostle saw them, in his vision's dream, 790
Arrayed for the wedding on that hill top,
The fair new city, Jerusalem.

lost in the translation. **784** The text continues to pun on **maskelles** *spotless*, and **makeles** *matchless, mateless*. The maiden is spotless, but she is a member of the company of 144 thousand virgins, brides of the Lamb. **786 flot** lit., *company, host. Flock*, however, though it would complete the alliteration on *f*, would give an approximate rhyme. MS gives **A hondred & forty** but not the **fowre** that G adds. **791 coppe** This is an approximate rhyme in the text also. Emerson emended it to **cot**, but H points out that **coppe** is the accepted MS reading. **792** Because of the limited number of rhymes for *Jerusalem*, the translators have used approximate rhymes here.

67

Of Jerusalem I in speche spelle
If þou wyl knaw what kyn he be
795 My lombe my Lorde my dere juelle
My ioy my blys my lemman fre
Þe profete Ysaye of hym con melle
Pitously of hys debonerte
Þat gloryous gyltleȝ þat mon con quelle
800 Wythouten any sake of felonye
As a schep to þe slaȝt þer lad watȝ he
& as lombe þat clypper in lande nem
So closed he hys mouth fro vch query
Quen Jueȝ hym iugged in Jerusalem

68

805 In Jerusalem watȝ my lemman slayn
& rent on rode wyth boyeȝ bolde
Al oure baleȝ to bere ful bayn
He toke on hymself oure careȝ colde
Wyth boffeteȝ watȝ hys face flayn
810 Þat watȝ so fayr on to byholde
For synne he set hymself in vayn
Þat neuer hade non hymself to wolde
For vus he lette hym flyȝe & folde
& brede vpon a bostwys bem
815 As meke as lomp þat no playnt tolde
For vus he swalt in Jerusalem

795 The minor accent rhyme appears also in the text. 802 The *lambs* are singular in the text. lande G, hande; Savage, honde. The translators have evaded the problem. The *l* is needed for alliteration. H, in lande[n]e[m] *seizes on heath.* 807 bayn *ready.* The translators have used *bane* for *bale.* 809 *like rain* is our addition for the rhyme.

67

"Of Jerusalem in speech I spell,
If thou wilt know what kind He be,
My Lamb, my Lord, my dear Jewel,   795
My Joy, my Bliss, my Belovèd free.
The prophet Isaiah of Him could tell,
Describing His meekness, compassionately:
Glorious, guiltless, whom man did fell,
Though there was no charge of felony.   800
Like a sheep to the slaughter led was He,
And like lambs when the shearer seizes them,
So He closed His mouth from each inquiry,
When the Jews judged Him in Jerusalem.

68

"In Jerusalem was my Belovèd slain   805
And rent on rood by ruffians bold;
He readily bore our grief and bane
And took on Himself our carkings cold,
While flaying buffets fell like rain
On His face that was once so fair to behold,   810
For our sins He counted His own life vain
And, sinless Himself, for sin was sold.
He suffered scourges darkly doled
On a rough cross stretched for requiem,
And meek as a lamb that no plaint told,   815
For us He died in Jerusalem.

---

811 The theology is not entirely clear here. He who did no sin **set hymself in vayn,** which H translates as *naught,* since the sacrifice was not in vain. **814** *requiem* The number of appropriate rhymes for *Jerusalem* is very limited.

69

Jerusalem Jordan & Galalye
Þer as baptysed þe goude saynt John
His wordeȝ acorded to Ysaye
820 When Jesus con to hym warde gon
He sayde of hym þys professye
Lo Godeȝ lombe as trwe as ston
Þat dotȝ away þe synneȝ dryȝe
Þat alle þys worlde hatȝ wroȝt vpon
825 Hymself ne wroȝt neuer ȝet non
Wheþer on hymself he con al clem
Hys generacyoun quo recen con
Þat dyȝed for vus in Jerusalem

70

In Jerusalem þus my lemman swatte
830 Twyeȝ for lombe watȝ taken þare
By trw recorde of ayþer prophete
For mode so meke & al hys fare
Þe þryde tyme is þerto ful mete
In Apokalypeȝ wryten ful ȝare
835 In mydeȝ þe trone þere saynteȝ sete
Þe apostel John hym saytȝ as bare
Lesande þe boke with leueȝ sware
Þere seuen syngnetteȝ wern sette in seme
& at þat syȝt vche douth con dare
840 In helle in erþe & Jerusalem

---

822 From this line onwards the *b* rhymes of *on* gave considerable trouble. **823** H, lit., *Who doth take away the iniquities.* The alliteration on *d* has been lost in translation. **824** The **vpon** is awkward, but it is in the text. O has a note on the amassing of sins through the ages. **826 con** does not mean *chose*, literally, and alliteration has been sacrificed for clarity. **clem** O, G, *claim;* H, *smear.* In the context of the passage, the translators think that the reference is to the taking on of the sins of mankind, with also a sense of *smear*, as O's note shows. **827 recen con** O, *tell in order;* G, H, *recount.* The translators are not certain of the meaning of *generation* in the context, but think it refers to human beings as the sons of God, who cannot truly understand the death and sacrifice of Christ. **829** MS, H, **swatte;** G, **swete.** **832 fare** G, O, *demeanor;* H, *ways,* from

69

"Jerusalem, Jordan, and Galilee,
Wherever baptized the good St. John,
His words and Isaiah's both agree.
When Jesus had toward him gone, 820
He spoke of Him this prophecy:
'Lo, true as stone, God's Lamb took on
Himself our sins' iniquity:
All the sins that this world has done,
Though He Himself did never one, 825
For Himself He chose to claim all of them.
His generation who has known
That died for us in Jerusalem?'

70

"In Jerusalem my Belovèd bled.
Twice as a Lamb He was taken there, 830
By the true account of each prophet,
His mood so meek wherever He fare.
The third time, equal, is not come yet,
As the Apocalypse does declare.
In the midst of the throne where the saints were set, 835
The Apostle John his words laid bare,
Leafing the Book with its leaves all square,
Where the seven seals were set on them.
And, at the sight, each soul was aware,
In hell, in earth, in Jerusalem. 840

the OE *faru*. Although the word in the text is surely a noun, the translators have used the verb, because they believe the description refers to His *demeanor* or *ways* wherever He *went*, from the OE *faran*. **833 mete** O, *properly;* G, *fitting;* H, *equal*. The translators think the sense is that the third account is equal or appropriate to the first two. Alliteration has been lost. **837 Lesande** O, G, H, *opening*. The translators did not want to lose the alliteration on *l*. **838 seme** O, with *in, together;* G, *border;* H, *line*. Probably *border* or *edge* makes best sense, but the rhymes for *Jerusalem* are few. **839 douth con dare** O, *people* or *creature tremble with fear;* G, *company, host cower with fear;* H, *each creature worshipped Him*. H's note refers to ll. 609-610. The translators think that in both places "fear" is in the sense of religious awe.

XV   71 *

Thys Jerusalem lombe hade neuer pechche
Of oþer huee bot quyt jolyf
Þat mot ne masklle moȝt on streche
For wolle quyte so ronk & ryf
845 Forþy vche saule þat hade neuer teche
Is to þat lombe a worthyly wyf
& þaȝ vch day a store he feche
Among vus commeȝ nonoþer strot ne stryf
Bot vchon enle we wolde were fyf
850 Þe mo þe myryer so God me blesse
In compayny gret our luf con þryf
In honour more & neuer þelesse

72

Lasse of blysse may non vus bryng
Þat beren þys perle vpon oure bereste
855 For þay of mote couþe neuer mynge
Of spotleȝ perleȝ þa beren þe creste
Alþaȝ oure corses in clotteȝ clynge
& ȝe remen for rauþe wythouten reste
We þurȝoutly hauen cnawyng
860 Of o[n] deth ful oure hope is drest
Þe lombe vus gladeȝ oure care is kest
He myrþes vus alle at vch a mes
Vchoneȝ blysse is breme & beste
& neuer oneȝ honour ȝet neuer þeles

* Stanzas 71-77 all end with similar terminal lines. Presumably one was to be cancelled in revision. O believes that stanza 72 is interpolated, since it adds nothing to the poem except the idea of the second death.

843 on streche O, *spread;* G, *rest upon;* H, *reach.* **844 ryf** probably a rhyme word, literally; O, G, H, *abundantly.* The alliteration on *r* has been lost in translation. **845** The translators have repeated *mark* (**teche** O, *stain, sin;* G, *stain, guilt;* H, *stain.* L. 841 has **pechche** O, *sin;* G, *fault, impurity;* H, *patch, shred*). **846** The alliteration on

XV   71 *

"This Jerusalem Lamb had never a mark
Of another hue but fairest white.
No blot or blemish made Him dark,
But all was white wool, rich and bright.
Therefore each soul without a mark   845
Is to the Lamb His spouse by right,
And though each day more souls embark,
We feel among us no stress or spite.
Were each one five, we should delight;
The more the merrier, God me bless!   850
In our great number love gains might,
In honor more and never the less.

72

"Less than bliss no memories bring,
Who bear His pearl upon our breast,
For they ignore all trifling   855
Who wear of spotless pearls the crest.
In clods the corpse lies mouldering;
Ye groan in grief and know no rest,
But we have knowledge of everything:
To the single death our hope addressed,   860
In the joy of the Lamb, by no death depressed.
At feasts He fills us with mirthfulness,
And each one's bliss is intensely blest,
Yet never one's honor any the less.

---

w is lost in the translation.   **847 he feche** O, *He fetch;* G, *bring in;* H, *fetch.*   **855 mynge** O, *speak of, call attention to;* G, *think of;* H, *be mindful of, be concerned.*   **856 creste** O, *the crown of pearls;* G, *ornament worn on the head;* H, *crest, top, best*—the idea that the best pearl is the Kingdom of Heaven. The translators have tried to keep both ideas.   **860** H believes this to be salvation from the "second death" of Judgment Day; G refers to salvation through the death of Christ. The first death is the death of the body; the second is the death of the soul. Revelation 2:11, 2:6, 14-15.   **861 kest** O, *cast out;* G, *removed;* H, *cast away.*

73

865 Lest les þou leue my tale farande
In Appocalyppece is wryten in wro
I seghe says John þa loumbe hym stande
On þe mount of Syon ful þryuen & þro
& wyth hym maydenneȝ an hundreþe þowsande
870 & fowre & forty þowsande mo
On alle her forhedeȝ wryten I fande
Þe lombeȝ nome hys fadereȝ also
A hue fro heuen I herde þoo
Lyk flodeȝ fele laden runnen on resse
875 & as þunder þroweȝ in torreȝ blo
Þat lote I leue watȝ neuer þe les

74

Nauþeles þaȝ hit schowted scharpe
& ledden loude alþaȝ hit were
A note ful nwe I herde hem warpe
880 To lysten þat watȝ ful lufly dere
As harporeȝ harpen in her harpe
Þat nwe songe þay songen ful cler
In sounande noteȝ a gentyl carpe
Ful fayre þe modeȝ þay fonge in fere
885 Ryȝt byfore Godeȝ chayere
& þe fowre besteȝ þat hym obes
& þe aldermen so sadde of chere
Her songe þay songen neuer þe les

866 in wro O, *place in book;* G, *nook, corner, passage;* H, *section, passage.* Translation of this stanza is difficult because of *b* rhymes. **875** The alliteration on þ is lost in translation. **879** *start* is not an accurate rhyme, but **warpe** is lost in NE and the number of available

73

"Lest my tale thou disbelieve,   865
In Apocalypse it is written clear:
'The Lamb,' says John, 'I could perceive
Stand brave on Zion's mount, and near
Him one hundred thousand maidens cleave.
Forty-four thousand more appear,   870
And on their foreheads all receive
The Lamb's name and His Father's. Here
A hue from Heaven reached my ear,
As the roar of many rivers press,
And as thunders roll in blue tors drear,   875
That sound I say was never the less.

74

" 'Nevertheless, though shouted sharp
And the lyric sound was loud to hear,
I heard them on a new note start,
Lovely to listen to and dear.   880
As harpers harp upon the harp,
The new-found song they sang out clear.
In resounding notes, in gentle carp,
The fair modes that they found cohere.
And right before God's throne, and near   885
The four beasts who His power confess,
The elders all with sober cheer
Sang their song, nevertheless.

rhymes is severely limited. **883 carpe** O, *a discourse;* G, H, *utter-ance.* The meaning has shifted somewhat; the translators could not solve the rhyme problem. **884 in fere** lit., *together.*

75

Nowþelese non watȝ neuer so quoynt
890 For alle þe crafteȝ þat euer þay knewe
Þat of þat songe myȝt synge a poynt
Bot þat meyny þe lombe þay swe
For þay arn boȝt fro þe vrþe aloynte
As newe fryt to God ful due
895 & to þe gentyl lombe hit arn anioynt
As lyk to hymself of lote & hwe
For neuer lesyng ne tale vntrwe
Ne towched her tonge for no dysstresse
Þat moteles meyny may neuer remwe
900 Fro þat maskeleȝ mayster neuer þe les

76

Neuer þe les let be my þonc
Quod I my perle þaȝ I appose
I schulde not tempte þy wyt so wlonc
To Krysteȝ chambre þat art ichose
905 I am bot mokke & mul among
& þou so ryche a reken rose
& bydeȝ here by þys blysful bonc
Þer lyueȝ lyste may neuer lose
Now hynde þat sympelnesse coneȝ enclose
910 I wolde þe aske a þynge expresse
& þaȝ I be bustwys as a blose
Let my bone vayl neuer þe lese

889 Nowþelese nothless, archaic form, in text. It has been adopted for the meter. **quoynt**—in the meaning of *skilled* has been lost. The translated line lacks the additional idea of "never" found in the text. **895 anioynt** lit., *joined;* O, *appointed;* G, H, *assigned, united.* **896 lote** O, *aspect;* G, *word, speech;* H, *appearance.* **899** The alliteration on *m* in this line and in the next is lost with the disappearance of **moteles** and **meyny** from the language. **901 þonc** O, *thought;* G, *thanks;* H, *pardon.* **903 wlonc** O, G, H, *fine, noble.* There is no room for the adjective in the rhymed translation. **þy wyt** lit., *thy wit,*

75

" 'Nathless, no one had skill so great
(For all the knowledge that ever they knew)   890
In that tune to participate
Except those who the Lamb pursue.
For they are redeemed from earth's estate,
The first fruits that to God fall due,
And with the Lamb associate,   895
Like to Himself in look and hue,
For never lying nor tale untrue
Touched their tongues, whatever the stress.'
That spotless company never withdrew
From that spotless Master, nevertheless."   900

76

"Nevertheless, pray pardon me,"
Quoth I, "my pearl, though I questions pose.
I should not try my wit with thee,
Whom Christ unto His chamber chose.
I am but muck and mold, you see,   905
And thou so rich and rare a rose!
O gracious in simplicity,
Who on this beautiful bank repose,
Abiding in bliss thou shalt never lose,
I would ask of thee a thing express,   910
Though churlish I am—I cannot gloze—
Let my prayer persuade thee, nevertheless.

but the translation using this form is not clear. **905 among** Savage, *in your company*. The translators have sacrificed this to meter. **906 reken** O, *radiant, fresh;* G, *fresh, gay;* H, *perfect*. H cites J. P. Oakden, *Alliterative Poetry in Middle English,* Publications of the University of Manchester, English Series, No. 22, Manchester, 1935: "a word of very lax application." **907-909** These lines have been transposed for the translation, in rhyme. **hynde** O, *gracious;* G, H, *gracious one*. **911 bustwys** O, *forward;* G, H, *rough, crude*. **blose** O, *flame;* G, not known in ME, *rough, uncouth person*(?); *H, dolt, clod*.

XVI   77

Neuer þe lese cler I yow bycalle
If ȝe con se hyt be to done
915 As þou art gloryous wythouten galle
Wythnay þou neuer my ruful bone
Haf ȝe no woneȝ in castel walle
Ne maner þer ȝe may mete & won
Þou tellez me of Jerusalem the ryche ryalle
920 Þer Dauid dere watȝ dyȝt on trone
Bot by þyse holteȝ hit con not hone
Bot in Judee hit is þat noble note
As ȝe ar maskeleȝ vnder mone
Your woneȝ schulde be wythouten mote

78

925 Þys moteleȝ meyny þou coneȝ of mele
Of þousandeȝ þryȝt so gret a route
A gret cete for ȝe arn fele
Yow byhod haue wythouten doute
So cumly a pakke of joly juele
930 Wer euel don schulde lyȝ þeroute
& by þyse bonkeȝ þer I con gele
& I se no bygyng nawhere aboute
I trowe alone ȝe lenge & loute
To loke on þe glory of þys grac[i]ous gote
935 If þou hatȝ oþer lygyngeȝ stoute
Now tech me to þat myry mote

---

914 Shifts between *you/thou* occur in the MS. The translators have tried to keep these shifts inconspicuous, though making use of them, also. **915 galle** O, *bitterness, rancor;* G, *spot of impurity;* H, *gall, blemish.* Difficult in NE. **917** Lit., *within the castle enclosure.* **920** Lit., *where David dear was established on throne.* **921 holteȝ** O, G, H, *groves.* **922 noble note** O, no glossary note; G, *piece of work, structure;* H, *piece of work, city.* **933 loute** O, *are*

XVI   77

"Nevertheless I clearly call
Thee, if thou canst fulfill it there;
As thou art glorious without gall,   915
Never refuse my piteous prayer.
Have ye no home within the wall,
No manor for meeting, anywhere?
The tale of Jerusalem, realm royal,
Dais of David, a regal chair,   920
Tells not of these groves. It is elsewhere;
In Judea it is, that princely plot.
As under the moon unmarred you are,
Your mansion should be without a spot.

78

"You speak of this spotless company,   925
Of thousands thronged, so great a rout.
A great city, for ye are many,
You ought to have, without a doubt,
A collection of jewels, bright and comely,
Endangered, should they lie without.   930
Yet by these banks where now I tarry,
I see no building hereabout.
I believe you linger alone and out
Upon this glory gaze; if not,
If you have other lodgings stout,   935
Direct me to that spritely spot."

hidden, live in retirement; G, *make one's way;* H, *bend.* This and the succeeding line are altered because of the loss of the words needed for the rhyme. **934 gote** O, G, H, *stream.* **935** G notes that the word must be **bygyngeʒ**, since ME **lygyngeʒ** "is not recorded elsewhere, and would normally denote a mere lodge or temporary shelter . . . hardly to be described as 'stout.'" The translators dislike *stout* in translation, but it appears as a rhyme word in the text.

79

That mote þou meneʒ in Judy londe
Þat specyal spyce þen to me spakk
Þat is þe cyte þat þe lombe con fonde
940 To soffer inne sor for maneʒ sake
Þe olde Jerusalem to vnderstonde
For þere þe olde gulte watʒ don to slake
Bot þe nwe þat lyʒt of Godeʒ sonde
Þe apostel in Apocallypce in theme con take
945 Þe lompe þer wythouten spotteʒ blake
Hatʒ feryed þyder hys fayre flote
& as hys flok is wythouten flake
So is hys mote wythouten moote

80

Of motes two to carpe clene
950 & Jerusalem hyʒt boþe nawþeles
Þat nys to yow no more to mene
Bot cete of God oþer syʒt of pes
In þat on oure pes watʒ mad at ene
Wyth payne to suffer þe lombe hit chese
955 In þat oþer is noʒt bot pes to glene
Þat ay schal laste wythouten reles
Þat is þe borʒ þat we to pres
Fro þat oure flesch be layd to rote
Þer glory & blysse schal euer encres
960 To þe meyny þat is wythouten mote

940-942 Ll. 940 and 942 have perfect rhyme in translation, but not in the text. **943 sonde** O, sending forth; G, *sending;* H, *command.* **946 fayre flote** lit., *fair flock.* The rhyme is a problem. **947** The original also plays on *flock* and *flake.* **948** The original text plays on the word **mote** as the translation plays on the word *spot.* **949 carpe clene** lit., *to speak exactly.* **951** The text is awkward; it has

79

"You speak of that spot in Judah's land,"
That peerless person then to me spake,
"That is the place where our Lord planned
To suffer sorely for mankind's sake.   940
In the old Jerusalem, understand,
The ancient sin He could forsake.
But the New ordained through God's command
The Apostle in Apocalypse could take
As theme. There the spotless Lamb could make   945
Thither His way with His lovely lot;
And, as His flock is without a flake,
So is His spot without a spot.

80

"Of the two spots, as can be seen,
Both are Jerusalem, nevertheless.   950
To you that name must simply mean
The 'City of God,' or 'Sight of Peace.'
In the one, our peace was made serene,
Where the Lamb chose pain with no release.
In the other is naught but peace to glean   955
That shall last forever without surcease.
That is the town toward which we press,
From the time our flesh is laid to rot.
There glory and bliss shall ever increase
For that assembly without a spot."   960

been translated literally. **952** Approximate *b* rhymes appear in the MS, but more of them have been used in the translation. **953 ene** O, *complete*; G, *arranged, settled*; H, *at one time, formerly*. The translators think it means *at one*, therefore O, G, *serene*. **954** H, *With pain to suffer, the Lamb did choose it.*

81

Motele₃ may so meke & mylde
Þen sayde I to þat lufly flor
Bryng me to þat bygly bylde
& let me se þy blysful bor
965 Þat schene sayde þat God wyl schylde
Þou may not enter wythinne hys tor
Bot of þe lombe I haue þe aquylde
For a sy₃t þerof þur₃ gret fauor
Vtwyth to se þat clene cloystor
970 Þou may bot inwyth not a fote
To strech in þe strete þou hat₃ no vygour
Bot þou wer clene wythouten mote

XVII   82

If I þis mote þe schal vnhyde
Bow vp towarde þys borne₃ heued
975 & I anende₃ þe on þis syde
Schal sve tyl þou to a hil be veued
Þen wolde [I] no lenger byde
Bot lurked by launce₃ so lufly leued
Tyl on a hyl þat I asspyed
980 & blusched on þe burghe as I forth dreued
By₃onde þe brok fro me warde keued
Þat schyrrer þen sunne wyth schafte₃ schon
In þe Apokalypce is þe fasoun preued
As deuyse₃ hit þe apostel Jhon

Þat schene sayde O, H, *that shining one said*; G, *that fair one said*. It has been omitted in the translation. *His words were bleak* has been added to the original to fill out the line. **967 aquylde** O, G, H, *obtained permission.* **968-969** Minor accent, approximate double rhymes are used in the text. **969-970** G, *From without you can see that radiant precinct, but from within not a foot.* The translators, however, agree with Gollancz that the permission is to see the city from outside but not to set one foot within. H, no note. **976-977** L. 976 runs on in the translation, so that *to a hill* comes in l. 977. **978** H's literal translation, *But stole on through the*

81

"Spotless maid, so mild and meek,"
Then said I to that lovely flower,
"To enter that bright abode I seek—
O let me see that blissful bower."
"That God forbade. His words were bleak: 965
Thou mayst not enter within His tower,
But of the Lamb I did bespeak
A sight thereof through His great favor:
From without to see that clean enclosure
Thou mayst; to go within, ask not;   970
To stand in that street, thou hast no power,
Unless thou art clean, without a spot.

XVII   82

"Should I this spot to thee confide,
Turn upwards toward this river's head,
And opposite to thee, on this side,   975
I shall follow, till thou art led
To a hill." No longer would I bide,
But, brushed by branches, with leaves unshed,
Till on a hill there I descried
And saw the city, as forth I sped.   980
Beyond the brook in its low bed,
Sheerer than shafts of sunlight, it shone.
In the Apocalypse, the way is read
As pictured by the Apostle John.

branches' so beautifully leaved'. The translators altered it somewhat
to preserve the alliteration and the rhyme. **980** The alliteration on
b has been lost, as **blusche** *look* is lost, and **burghe** *burg* now has a
poor connotation. **981 warde keued** O, *plunged toward;* O uses MS
breued *seen;* G, **keued** *sunk down, Sunk down (from Heaven) on
the other side of the brook from me.* H, *low-placed,* not to modify
the brook, as it has been translated here, but the New Jerusalem
(Apocalypse 21:2, 10-11) "descended, sunk down from heaven."
982 There are 4 stressed *s*'s in the text.

83

985 As John þe apostel hit syȝ wyth syȝt
I syȝe þat cyty of gret renoun
Jerusalem so nwe & ryally dyȝt
As hit watȝ lyȝt fro þe heuen adoun
Þe borȝ watȝ al of brende golde bryȝt
990 As glemande glas burnist broun
Wyth gentyl gemmeȝ anvnder pyȝt
Wyth banteleȝ twelue on basyng boun
Þe foundementeȝ twelue of riche tenoun
Vch tabelment watȝ a serlypeȝ ston
995 As derely deuysez þis ilk toun
In Apocalyppeȝ þe apostel John

84

As [John] þise stoneȝ in writ con nemme
I knew þe name after his tale
Jasper hyȝt þe fyrst gemme
1000 Þat I on þe fyrst basse con wale
He glente grene in þe lowest hemme
Saffer helde þe secounde stale
Þe calsydoyne þenne wythouten wemme
In þe þryd table con purly pale
1005 Þe emerade þe furþe so grene of scale
Þe sardonyse þe fyfþe ston
Þe sexte þe rybe he con hit wale
In þe Apocalyppce þe apostel John

988 H thinks this line parallels l. 981. The translators do not agree.
990 H, *Like gleaming crystal burnished bright.* **992 banteleȝ** O,
meaning not clear, part of the foundation; G, **bantels** *projecting
horizontal coursings;* H, **bantels,** no translation. **993 tenoun** O,
joining, construction; G, "having elaborately adorned tenons," *join-
ing;* H, *joining,* with note, "identical with the tiers of the founda-
tion." The alliteration on *t* has been lost in translation with the loss
of **tenoun. 999** The alliteration on *j* is lost in the translation.

83

Like John the Apostle, with vision's sight,   985
I saw that city much renowned:
Jerusalem new and royally dight,
As from the heavens descended. Round
The city burnished gold was bright
As crystal coruscating. Found   990
Beneath were precious gems; upright
Were pillars twelve on bases bound.
The twelve foundations were richly crowned
And every tier was a separate stone,
As deftly describes this holy ground,   995
In the Apocalypse, the Apostle John.

84

As Scripture gave these stones a name,
By John's account, these names I knew:
Jasper first in order came,
On the first foundation it was in view,   1000
Green it gleamed on the lowest frame.
In the second place was sapphire blue,
Chalcedony then without a stain,
In the third place, pale till the light shone through.
The emerald fourth, so green of hue,   1005
The sardonyx fifth was set thereon;
The sixth the ruby he pointed to,
In the Apocalypse, the Apostle John.

1000 wale O, G, H, *discern.* **1001 hemme** O, *hem,* "used loosely (for rime?) for the first tier in the foundation of the New Jerusalem"; G, *projecting edge (forming step)*; H, *border.* **1003** G's note on *chalcedony* from the OED, "having the lustre nearly of wax, and being either transparent or translucent." **1004 purly pale** O, *appeared pale in purity;* G, *show pale and clear;* H, *translucently paled.* **1006** The alliteration on *s* is in the stressed position of *sardonyx.*

85

ȝet joyned John þe crysolyt
1010 Þe seuenþe gemme in fundament
Þe aȝtþe þe beryl cler & quyt
Þe topasye twynne-how þe nente endent
Þe crysopase þe tenþe is tyȝt
Þe jacyngh þe eleuenþe gent
1015 Þe twelþe þe gentyleste in vch a plyt
Þe amatyst purpre wyth ynde blente
Þe wal abof þe bantels bent
O jasporye as glas þat glysnande schon
I knew hit by his deuysement
1020 In þe Apocalyppeȝ þe apostel John

86 *

As John deuysed ȝet saȝ I þare
Þise twelue degres wern brode & stayre
Þe cyte stod abof ful sware
As longe as brode as hyȝe ful fayre
1025 Þe streteȝ of golde as glasse al bare
Þe wal of jasper þat glent as glayre
Þe woneȝ wythinne enurned ware
Wyth alle kynneȝ perre þat moȝt repayre
Þenne helde vch sware of þis manayre
1030 Twelue forlonge space er euer hit fon
Of heȝt of brede of lenþe to cayre
For meten hit syȝ þe apostel John

1013 **tyȝt** O, *came;* G, note, *connected, fastened,* an architectural use, also H. The alliteration on *t* is lost in the translation. **1017 bantels** See note on l. 992. **bent** G, *bound, fastened;* O's note says to supply **watȝ** or **set;** H, *extended.* The alliteration on *b* is lost in the translation.

* The *a* and *b* rhymes are the same, "are," throughout this stanza. The translation follows the text.

85

To these John joined the chrysolite,
The seventh gem set in the base,   1010
The eighth the beryl clear and white,
The twin-hued topaz ninth in place,
The chrysoprase the tenth in sight,
The jacinth the eleventh grace,
The twelfth, the noblest in every plight,   1015
The amethyst purple and blue embrace.
The wall above the pillars' face,
Of jasper, glass-like, glistening, shone.
From the Apocalypse I could trace
What he portrayed, the Apostle John.   1020

86 *

As John described, I, too, saw where
These twelve tiers formed a steep, broad flare.
The city stood above, four-square,
As long as broad as high, and fair:
Of gold like glass, the streets—all bare;   1025
The walls of jasper gleamed like glair;
The dwellings within were adorned and there
All sorts of stones, a gathering rare.
Within this city each section's share
Twelve furlongs' space ere it was done.   1030
Of height and breadth and length did declare
This marvel's measure, the Apostle John.

1022 There is no *flare* in the MS. The translation is *broad* and
steep. The problem is with the rhyme. 1023 sware O, *square;* G,
H, *foursquare.* 1029 sware O, *side of a square;* G, *square;* H,
foursquare. 1031 cayre O, *make square;* G, *traverse,* note: "Since
the city is cubic in form, each side is a square." H, *to go, to reach.*
The translators have tried to avoid disputed meanings.

XVIII   87

As John hym wryteʒ ʒet more I syʒe
Vch pane of þat place had þre ʒateʒ
1035 So twelue in pourseut I con asspye
Þe portaleʒ pyked of rych plateʒ
& vch ʒate of a margyrye
A parfyt perle þat neuer fateʒ
Vchon in scrypture a name con plye
1040 Of Israel barneʒ folewande her dateʒ
Þat is to say as her byrþ whateʒ
Þe aldest ay fyrst þeron watʒ done
Such lyʒt þer lemed in alle þe strateʒ
Hem nedde nawþer sunne ne mone

88

1045 Of sunne ne mone had þay no nede
Þe self God watʒ her lombe lyʒt
Þe lombe her lantyrne wythouten drede
Þurʒ hym blysned þe borʒ al bryʒt
Þurʒ woʒe & won my lokyng ʒede
1050 For sotyle cler noʒt lette no lyʒt
Þe hyʒe trone þer moʒt ʒe hede
Wyth alle þe apparaylmente vmbepyʒte
As John þe appostel in termeʒ tyʒte
Þhe hyʒe Godeʒ self hit set vpone
1055 A reuer of þe trone þer ran outryʒte
Watʒ bryʒter þen boþe þe sunne & mone

1038 **þat neuer fateʒ** O, G, H, *that never fades.* 1041 **whateʒ** O,
was, that is, where their births were; G, H, *according to the fortunes
of their births.* 1046 Ll. 1046 and 1050 use identical rhyme in the
text. 1047 **wythouten drede** lit., *without doubt.* 1049 The loss of

XVIII   87

As John himself writes, more saw I:
Three gates each side of that estate,
So twelve in all I could espy,   1035
Each portal adorned with precious plate.
Each gate one pearl did occupy,
A perfect pearl inviolate.
On each the names identify
The sons of Israel by their date,   1040
(That is to say, whatever their fate),
The oldest first was placed thereon.
Those streets such light illuminate
They needed neither sun nor moon.

88

Of sun nor moon they had no need: 1045
God Himself was their lamp light;
The Lamb their lantern was indeed,
Through Him the city shone all bright.
Through house and hall could my gaze proceed,
For, subtly clear, naught stopped the light   1050
There the high throne you might heed,
The heavenly hosts above this sight.
As John the Apostle did truly write,
The High God's Self sat thereupon;
From the throne a river ran outright,   1055
Brighter than both the sun and moon.

ȝede *went* from NE makes translation difficult. **1052 vmbepyȝte** O, G, *adorned, round about;* H, *ranged about.* **1053 tyȝte** O, *described;* G, *set forth;* H, *expounded.* The alliteration on *t* is lost in the translation.

89

Sunne ne mone schon neuer so swete
A þat foysoun flode out of þat flet
Swyþe hit swange þurʒ vch a strete
1060 Wythouten fylþe oþer galle oþer glet
Kyrk þerinne watʒ non ʒete
Chapel ne temple þat euer watʒ set
Þe Almyʒty watʒ her mynster mete
Þe lombe þe sakerfyse þer to reget
1065 Þe ʒateʒ stoken watʒ neuer ʒet
Bot euermore vpen at vche a lone
Þer entreʒ non to take reset
Þat bereʒ any spot anvnder mone

90

The mone may þerof acroche no myʒte
1070 To spotty ho is of body to grym
& also þer ne is neuer nyʒt
What schulde þe mone þer compas clym
& to euen wyth þat worþly lyʒt
Þat schyneʒ vpon þe brokeʒ brym
1075 Þe planeteʒ arn in to pouer a plyʒt
& þe self sunne ful fer to dym
Aboute þat water arn tres ful schym
Þat twelue fryteʒ of lyf con bere ful sone
Twelue syþeʒ on ʒer þay beren ful frym
1080 & renowleʒ nwe in vche a mone

1058 flet O, noun, *ground;* G, *floor, ground,* (of the city); H, verb, *floated,* as in Apocalypse 22:1 "proceeding from the throne of God and of the Lamb." The translators have used the verb. 1061 ʒete O, G, H, *nevertheless, yet.* 1064 to reget O, *to reproduce* (the Mass will be offered in Heaven); G, refet, not the sense of "redeemed" but "worship and the soul's refreshment"; *the Lamb, the sacrifice, was there as refreshment;* H, *to redeem,* but there is no Mass in Heaven, Apocalypse 5:6, "A Lamb standing, as if slain." Verse 9 further supports the reading "redeem." 1066 at vche a lone

89

Never shone sun nor moon so sweet
As from the throne the full flood spilt,
Swiftly it swirled through every street,
Free from scum or slime or silt.   1060
No church therein, but yet complete—
No chapel or temple was ever built:
The Almighty was their minster meet,
And the Lamb was there to redeem all guilt.
The gates asunder ever wilt   1065
Be, never fastened from noon to noon.
None enters there for refuge who still
Bears any stain beneath the moon.

90

The moon therefrom may draw no might,
Too spotty it is, of body grim;   1070
Moreover, therein it is never night.
Why should the moon its compass rim
To level with that valued light
That shines upon the brooklet's brim?
The planets are too poor in plight;   1075
The sun itself is far too dim.
The water's edge the bright trees trim;
Twelve fruits of life they bear and soon,
Twelve times a year, with laden limb,
Renewed anew in every moon.   1080

lit., *always open at every lane*. The translators had difficulty with
the rhyme because of vowel changes. **1070 grym** O, *ugly;* G, *grim,
ugly;* H, *crude.* **1072 compas clym** O, G, H, *circuit climb.* The
translators recognize that this description of the everlasting light
of Heaven is difficult to follow. It is also difficult in the text. **1078
sone** *soon* and is so translated, although it appears to be a word
used for the sake of rhyme. **1080** Redundant expression is present
also in the text.

91

An vnder mone so gret merwayle
No fleschly hert ne myȝt endeure
As quen I blusched vpon þat baly
So ferly þerof watȝ þe fasure
1085 I stod as stylle as dased quayle
For ferly of þat freuch fygure
Þat felde I nawþer reste ne trauayle
So watȝ I rauyste wyth glymme pure
For I dar say wyth conciens sure
1090 Hade bodyly burne abiden þat bone
Þaȝ alle clerkeȝ hym hade in cure
His lyf wer lost an vnder mone

XIX   92

Ryȝt as þe maynful mone con rys
Er þenne þe day-glem dryue al doun
1095 So sodanly on a wonder wyse
I watȝ war of a prosessyoun
Þis noble cite of ryche enpresse
Watȝ sodanly ful wythouten sommoun
Of such vergyneȝ in þe same gyse
1100 Þat watȝ my blysful anvnder croun
& coronde wern alle of þe same fasoun
Depaynt in perleȝ & wedeȝ qwyte
In vchoneȝ breste watȝ bounden boun
Þe blysful perle wythouten delyt

1081 Elliptical construction is also in text. 1082 Lit., double nega-
tive **no . . . ne.** 1084 **fasure** O, *appearance;* G, *fashion;* H, *fash-
ioning.* The word is lost and the translators were confronted with a
problem of rhyme. 1086 **freuch fygure** O, *frail vision;* H, *noble
scene;* G, **frelich fygure,** *noble apparition.* In the translation the
meaning has been distorted for the rhyme. 1087 **trauayle** O, *labor;*
G, H, *toil.* 1091 *cure* is used in the sense of "cure of souls," as
the word is used in the text. 1096 **I watȝ war** lit., *I was aware.*
1098 **wythouten sommoun** has been omitted in the translation. In

91

Beneath the moon a marvel so great
No human heart might it endure.
My eyes were stayed on that estate,
So wondrous was that land's allure.
Like a dazèd quail I stood to wait—   1085
That marvel did my mind assure,
Until I felt no rest or weight,
So rapt was I in radiance pure.
For I dare say with conscience sure,
Could mortal man abide that boon,   1090
Though all the clerks had him in cure,
His life were lost beneath the moon.

XIX   92

Just as the mighty moon doth rise,
Ere droppeth down the gleam of day,
So suddenly in wondrous wise,   1095
I saw a procession wend its way.
This noble city of rich emprise
Had suddenly a full array
Of virgins all in the same guise
As did my blessèd one display,   1100
And all were crowned in the same way,
Adorned in pearl and raiment white.
On each one's breast serenely lay
The blessèd pearl of great delight.

---

modern English this crowds the line. It is implied in the **sodanly.**
1100 anvnder croun lit., *under her crown.* **1103 bounden boun** O,
fastened, no translation for **boun. boun** G, *fixed;* H, *fixed the
destined.* **1104** MS is illegible but the word is probably **wythouten.**
O interpolates [**gret**]. G gives **gret.** H uses **wythouten** and translates
it as *beyond.* No one indicates the problem in notes. Since **gret** is
the key word throughout stanzas 92-97 and is clear in all the other
lines, the translators believe that **wythouten** is a scribal error for
gret.

93

1105 Wyth gret delyt þay glod in fere
On golden gateȝ þat glent as glasse
Hundreth þowsandeȝ I wot þer were
& alle in sute her liureȝ wasse
Tor to knaw þe gladdest chere
1110 Þe lombe byfore con proudly passe
Wyth horneȝ seuen of red glod cler
As praysed perleȝ his wedeȝ wasse
Towarde þe throne þay trone a tras
Þaȝ þay wern fele no pres in plyt
1115 Bot mylde as maydeneȝ seme at mas
So droȝ þay forth wyth gret delyt

94

Delyt þat hys come encroched
To much hit were of for to melle
Þise aldermen quen he aproched
1120 Grouelyng to his fete þay felle
Legyounes of aungeleȝ togeder uoched
Þer kesten ensens of swete smelle
Þen glory & gle watȝ nwe abroched
Al songe to loue þat gay juelle
1125 Þe steuen moȝt stryke þurȝ vrþe to helle
Þat þe vertues of heuen of joye endyte
To loue þe lombe his meyny in melle
Iwysse I laȝt a gret delyt

1105 **in fere** O, *together;* G, H, *company.* The word is lost in NE.
1107 The alliteration on *w* is lost in the translation. 1108 **wasse**
is used in both ll. 1108 and 1112 in the text. 1109 The rhyme in
the translation is approximate, but *cheer* has inappropriate con-
notations in NE. 1112 First half of the line in the text alliterates
on *p*, the second on *w*. 1113 **tras** O, *course, way;* G, *made their
way, proceeded;* H, *train, retinue.* 1114 **plyt** O, *condition;* G, H

93

With great delight they glided, fair,　　　　　　　1105
On golden streets that gleamed like glass:
There were a hundred thousand there,
And all alike their livery was.
Hard to know the happiest here!
The Lamb in front did proudly pass,　　　　　　　1110
With seven horns of red-gold, clear.
Like precious pearls His raiment was.
Toward the throne they trod, and as
So many went, none pressed in plight,
But mild as maidens seem at Mass,　　　　　　　　1115
So they led on with great delight.

94

To them the Lamb, approaching, brought
Delight too great for me to tell:
The elders, at the sight, distraught
And prostrate at His feet they fell,　　　　　　　1120
And legions of His angels sought
To spread incense of sweetest smell;
Glory and gladness were new wrought;
All sang to praise that radiant jewel.
The sounds must strike through earth to hell,　　1125
And Heaven's virtues with joy recite,
Amid the many, His praises tell.
In truth I felt a great delight.

plight. **1116 droʒ** O, H, *drew, moved;* G, *proceeded.* **1117** The alliteration on *k* is lost in the translation. **1118 melle** O, *to talk, discourse;* G, H, *speak, tell.* **1120 grouelyng** O, G, H, *prostrate.* **1122 þer kesten** O, G, H, *to scatter.* **1124 juelle** Two of the translators indicate a possible pun on *Jew* plus the Hebrew *el,* meaning *place.* **1127 melle** See l. 1118. **1128 laʒt** O, H, *experienced;* G, *took.*

95

Delit þe lombe for to deuise
1130 Wyth much meruayle in mynde went
Best watȝ, he blyþest & moste to pryse
Þat euer I herde of speche spent
So worþyly whyt wern wedeȝ hys
His lokeȝ symple hymself so gent
1135 Bot a wounde ful wyde & weete con wyse
Anende hys hert þurȝ hyde torente
Of hys quyte syde his blod outsprent
Alas þoȝt I who did þat spyt
Ani breste for bale aȝt haf forbrent
1140 Er he þerto hade had delyt

96

The lombe delyt non lyste to wene
Þaȝ he were hurt & wounde hade
In his sembelaunt watȝ neuer sene
So wern his glenteȝ gloryous glade
1145 I loked among his meyny schene
How þay wyth lyf wern laste & lade
Þen saȝ I þer my lyttel quene
Þat I wende had standen by me in sclade
Lorde much of mirþe watȝ þat ho made
1150 Among her fereȝ þat watȝ so quyt
Þat syȝt me gart to þenk to wade
For luf-longyng in gret delyt.

1134 The alliteration on *s* is lost in the translation. **1135 wyse** O,
G, *appear;* H, *extend, run.* **1141 wene** O, G, *doubt;* H, *think,
imagine.* O, noun (*Yet*) *it would please none to doubt the Lamb's
joy.* H, noun *It is impossible to imagine the Lamb's delight. All the*

95

Delight the Lamb to contemplate,
My mind there in amazement went.   1130
Best was He, blithest, ultimate
On whom I ever heard speech spent.
Gloriously white His garments' state,
His looks serene, beneficent,
But a wide wound, and wet, in spate,   1135
Beneath His heart, through skin sore rent,
From His white side the blood besprent.
Whoever, thought I, wreaked that spite,
His breast should burn and he repent,
Before therein he took delight.   1140

96

Let none the Lamb's delight demean,
Though He were hurt, with fierce wounds flayed,
In His semblance it was never seen—
Gladness His glorious looks conveyed.
I looked among His company sheen,   1145
How they abundant life displayed,
And there I saw my little queen
Whom I thought with me in the glade.
Lord, much merriment she made
Among her friends, all dressed in white.   1150
That sight caused me to want to wade
Toward her, love-longing in delight.

other translators express the idea of "doubt." **1146 laste & lade**
O, G, *loaded and laden.* **1148** The alliteration on *s* is lost in the
translation.

XX   97

Delyt me drof in yȝe & ere
My maneȝ mynde to maddyng malte
1155 Quen I seȝ my frely I wolde be þere
Byȝonde þe water þaȝ ho were walte
I þoȝt þat noþyng myȝt me dere
To fech me bur & take me halte
& to start in þe strem schulde non me stere
1160 To swymme þe remnaunt þaȝ I þer swalte
Bot of þat munt I watȝ bitalt
When I schulde start in þe strem astraye
Out of þat caste I watȝ bycalt
Hit watȝ not at my prynceȝ paye

98

1165 Hit payed hym not þat I so flonc
Ouer meruelous mereȝ so mad arayde
Of raas þaȝ I were rasch & ronk
Ȝet rapely þerinne I watȝ restayed
For ryȝt as I sparred vnto þe bonc
1170 Þat brathe out of my drem me brayde
Þen wakned I in þat erber wlonk
My hede vpon þat hylle watȝ layde
Þer as my perle to grounde strayd
I raxled & fel in gret affray
1175 & sykyng to myself I sayd
Now al be to þat prynceȝ paye

1156 Alliteration on *w* is lost. **walte** O, *kept;* G, *cast, set;* H, *vexed*—
the maiden would be vexed at the jeweler's crossing; Savage, *walled.*
The translators think the dreamer believes he must go to her since she
will *stay* where she is.   **1158** This translation follows G, although
Gollancz argues for success *if no one prevented the . . . take-off.*

XX   97

Delight rushed in through eye and ear.
My mind to madness then gave way.
When I saw my sweet, I would be near,   **1155**
Though she across the stream would stay.
I thought that I had naught to fear,
To keep me back, my start delay;
To cross the stream my way seemed clear:
To swim the rest, though death me slay.   **1160**
But that resolve was turned astray,
When into the stream I tried to spring,
From that attempt I was torn away:
It was not the pleasure of my King.

98

It pleased Him not that I should dash   **1165**
Over that marvelous mere. Arrayed
In madness I rushed, both proud and rash,
Yet swiftly therein I was stayed.
Just as I charged the bank, that brash
Violence broke my dream and made   **1170**
Me wake in the garden. In a flash
My head upon that hill was laid
Where into the ground my pearl had strayed.
I roused, in wretched shuddering,
And, to myself, I said, dismayed: **1175**
"Be all the pleasure of the King."

H, *to work up speed for myself* and for **take me halte,** lit. *spring high,*
or *betake me,* or *take myself high.* **1159 stere** O, *prevent;* G, *re-*
strain, but may be error for **skere** *frighten off.* See the MS. **1170**
The alliteration on *b* is lost.

99 *

Me payed ful ille to be outfleme
So sodenly of þat fayre regioun
Fro alle þo syȝteȝ so quyke & queme
1180 A longeyng heuy me strok in swone
     & rewfully þenne I con to reme
     O perle quod I of rych renoun
     So watȝ hit me dere þat þou con deme
     In þys veray avysyoun
1185 If hit be ueray & soth sermoun
     Þat þou so stykeȝ in garlande gay
     So wel is me in þys doel-doungoun
     Þat þou art to þat prynces paye

100

To þat prynces paye hade I ay bente
1190 & ȝerned no more þen watȝ me geuen
     & halden me þer in trwe entent
     As þe perle me prayed þat watȝ so þryuen
     As helde drawen to Goddeȝ present
     To mo of his mysterys I hade ben dryuen
1195 Bot ay wolde man of happe more hente
     Þen moȝten by ryȝt vpon hem clyuen
     Þefore my ioye watȝ sone toriuen
     & I kaste of kyþeȝ þat lasteȝ aye
     Lorde mad hit arn þat agayn þe stryuen
1200 Oþer proferen þe oȝt agayn þy paye

---

* Four of the *b* rhymes in this stanza use minor accent: **regioun,**
avysyoun, sermoun, and **doungoun.** These have been followed in
the translation.

1185 sermoun O, *saying;* G, *speech, account;* H, *teaching.* **1186**

99 *

It pleased me ill to be cast out
So suddenly from that fair region,
From visions vivid and dear about
Me. Longing struck like a heavy swoon   1180
And, ruefully, in voice devout,
"O pearl," quoth I, "of rich renown,
So dear to me, beyond a doubt,
Thou hast revealed a very vision.
If it be teaching true, thy sermon,   1185
That thou art set in His garland's ring,
I am wholly well in this doleful dungeon,
Since thou art the pleasure of the King."

100

To that King's pleasure was I bent
And craved no more than I was given;   1190
I held me there with true intent
As thou besought me, Pearl of Heaven.
But wilfully toward God I went;
To delve His mysteries I was driven;
For more good fortune would men augment   1195
Than belongs to them by right. Even
So my joy from me was riven:
I was hurled from realms unperishing.
Lord, mad are they who with Thee have striven,
Or displeased Thee in their proffering.   1200

G, H, the garland is the circle of the blessed, as in Dante. **1189** The
alliteration on *p* is lost. **1192** The alliteration on *p* is lost. **1198**
The alliteration on *k* is lost. **1200** This line has the word **paye,** but
does not follow the repeated line of the group which includes
prynce3 paye. proferen is the word in the text.

101

To pay þe Prince oþer sete saȝte
Hit is ful eþe to þe god Krystyin
For I haf founden hym boþe day & naȝte
A God a Lorde a frende ful fyin

1205 Ouer þis hyul þis lote I laȝte
For pyty of my perle enclyin
& syþen to God I hit bytaȝte
In Krysteȝ dere blessyng & myn
Þat in þe forme of bred & wyn

1210 Þe preste vus scheweȝ vch a daye
He gef vus to be his homly hyne
Ande precious perleȝ vnto his pay Amen. Amen.

1204 fyin O, *true;* G, *excellent, of the noblest;* H, *noble.*   **1205 lote**
G, probably *lot, fortune,* though it may be *utterance* or *song* (re-

101

To please the King or peaceful be
The Christian may with ease divine,
For day and night He is to me
God, Lord, and Friend, noble and fine.
On this hill I learned my destiny.   1205
Prostrate, I mourned the pearl, once mine,
And then to God, in memory,
To Christ's dear blessing, I resign
It to Him, whom bread and wine
Each day our priests reveal and bring.   1210
As His dear servants God assigns
Us, precious pearls unto the King. Amen, Amen.

ferring to the *Pearl* poem); H, *lot, destiny.* **1207 bytaȝte** O,
yielded up; G, *committed;* H, *gave up.*

Selected bibliography

SELECTED BIBLIOGRAPHY

This is a working bibliography of editions, translations, and articles referred to by the translators. It is not, of course, inclusive, since a full scholarly bibliography is beyond the scope of a Crofts Classics book.

EDITIONS AND TRANSLATIONS

Cawley, A. C., ed., *Pearl. Sir Gawain and the Green Knight* (London, Dent; New York, E. P. Dutton; Everyman Library, 1962).

Chase, Stanley Perkins, *The Pearl, the Fourteenth Century English Poem Rendered in Modern Verse with an Introductory Essay* (New York, Oxford University Press, 1932).

Coulton, G. C., *Pearl, a Fourteenth Century Poem Rendered into Modern English*, 2nd ed. (London, David Nutt, 1907).

Gollancz, Sir Israel, *Pearl, an English Poem of the Fourteenth Century, Edited with a Modern Rendering* (London, David Nutt, 1891).

Gollancz, Sir Israel, *Pearl, an English Poem of the XIVth Century, Edited with Modern Rendering, Together with Boccaccio's Olympia* (London, Oxford University Press, 1921).

Gordon, E. V., ed., *Pearl* (Oxford, Clarendon Press, 1953).

Hillman, Sr. Mary Vincent, *The Pearl, Mediaeval Text with a Literal Translation and Interpretation* (College of St. Elizabeth Press, New York, University Publishers, Inc., 1961).

Jewett, Sophie, *The Pearl, a Middle English Poem; a Modern Version in the Metre of the Original* (New York, T. Y. Crowell & Co., 1908).

Mead, Marian, *The Pearl, an English Vision Poem of the Fourteenth Century Done into Modern Verse* (Portland, Maine, Thomas B. Mosher, 1908).

Mitchell, S. Weir, *Pearl, Rendered into Modern English Verse* (Portland, Maine, Thomas B. Mosher; The Bibelot, 1908).

Osgood, Charles C., ed., *The Pearl, a Middle English Poem* (Boston, D. C. Heath & Co., 1906).

Osgood, Charles C., *Pearl, an Anonymous English Poem of the Fourteenth Century, Rendered in Prose* (Princeton, N.J., The Translator, 1907).

INTERPRETATION AND CRITICISM

Emerson, O. F., "Imperfect Lines in *Pearl* and in the Rimed Parts of *Sir Gawain and the Green Knight*," *Modern Philology*, XIX (1921-22), 131-141.

Emerson, O. F., "Some Notes on *The Pearl*," *Publications of the Modern Language Association of America*, XXXVII (1922), 52-93.

Emerson, O. F., "More Notes on *The Pearl*," *Publications of the Modern Language Association of America*, XLII (1927), 807-831.

Bishop, Ian, "The Significance of the 'Garlande Gay' in the Allegory of Pearl," *Review of English Studies*, VII (1957), 12-21.

Hamilton, Marie P., "The Meaning of the Middle English *Pearl*," *Publications of the Modern Language Association*, LXXV (1955), 805-825.

Hamilton, Marie P., "Notes on *Pearl*," *The Journal of English and Germanic Philology*, LVII (1958), 177-191.

Hillman, Sr. Mary Vincent. "*Pearl*, 382: mare reȝ mysse?" *Modern Language Notes*, LXVIII (1953), 528-531.

Hillman, Sr. Mary Vincent, "Some Debatable Words in *Pearl* and Its Theme," *Modern Language Notes*, LX (1945), 241-248.

Holman, C. Hugh, " 'Mareȝ Mysse' in *The Pearl*," *Modern Language Notes*, LXVI (1951), 33-36.

Kellogg, Alfred L., "Note on Line 274 on the 'Pearl,' " *Traditio*, XII (1956), 406 f.

Savage, Henry L., Review of Edition by Sr. Mary Vincent Hillman, *Speculum*, XXXIX, 1 (1964), 155-159.

Wright, E. M., "Notes on *Pearl*," wrongly entitled "Additional

Notes on *Sir Gawain and the Green Knight,*" *The Journal of English and Germanic Philology,* XXXVIII (1939), 1 ff.

Wright, E. M., "Additional Notes on the *Pearl,*" *The Journal of English and Germanic Philology,* XXXIX (1940), 315 ff.

Note: The new translation by John Gardner, *The Complete Works of the Gawain Poet,* Chicago, 1965, reached the translators too late to be used.